Edward Arber, John Earle

Micro-Cosmographie

Editio Princeps, 1628

Edward Arber, John Earle

Micro-Cosmographie
Editio Princeps, 1628

ISBN/EAN: 9783337172626

Printed in Europe, USA, Canada, Australia, Japan

Cover: Foto ©ninafisch / pixelio.de

More available books at **www.hansebooks.com**

English Reprints.

JOHN EARLE, M.A.

Fellow of Merton College, Oxford.

MICRO-COSMOGRAPHIE.

Editio princeps, 1628.

WITH ADDITIONAL CHARACTERS FROM THE FIFTH
EDITION OF 1629; AND THE SIXTH EDITION OF 1633.

CAREFULLY EDITED BY

EDWARD ARBER,

Affociate, King's College, London, F.R.G.S., &c.

LONDON:
5. QUEEN SQUARE, BLOOMSBURY, W.C.

Ent Stat. Hall.]   1 December, 1868.   [*All Rights referved.*

CONTENTS.

CHRONICLE of the Life, Works, and Times of J. Earle	3
INTRODUCTION	7
BIBLIOGRAPHY (1) Introductory	10
(2) Title-pages [reduced] of the second and third editions of 1628	11
(3) Issues during the Author's life time	12—15
(4) Issues fince the Author's death	16
MICRO-COSMOGRAPHIE, &c. 1628	17
(1) To the Reader Gentile or Gentle	18
(2) A Table of Contents	19—20
MICRO-COSMOGRAPHIE OR, A PIECE OF THE WORLD CHARACTERIZ'D	21

ADDITIONAL CHARACTERS,

Twenty-three now first found in Fifth Edition, 1629, but which may have been included in the fourth Edition, of which no copy is at present known.

One first found in the Sixth Edition, 1633 . . . 163

CHRONICLE

of

some of the principal events

in the

LIFE, WORKS, and TIMES

of

JOHN EARLE, M.A. [created in 1642 D.D.],

Fellow of Merton College, Oxford.

Subsequently, in succession, Rector of Bishopston, Wilts; Chaplain to Charles, Prince of Wales; Chancellor of the Diocese of Salisbury: an exile on the Continent; Clerk of the Closet to King Charles II.; Dean of Westminster; Bishop of Worcester; and Bishop of Salisbury.

---

* Probable or approximate dates.

1558. Nov. 17. Elizabeth begins to reign.

Birth. {
1600.* — JOHN EARLE received his first being in this vain and transitory world within the city of York. *Wood. Ath. Oxon. iii.* 716. *Ed.* 1817. "*John Earles*, Son of *Tho. Earles* Gent. sometime Register of the Arch-bishop's Court at *York*," [*see* 1660] is born. The date is fixed by his age, *Ætatis suæ* 65 *to*, at his death on 17 Nov. 1665, as inscribed on his monument in Merton College Chapel. These two quotations illustrate the uncertain spelling of his name: which was apparently written indifferently, with or without the 's.'

1603. Mar. 24. James I. succeeds to the English throne.

At Oxford. {
1608. — Bp. Hall's *Characters of Vertues and Vices* published.
1616. Mar. F. Beaumont the poet dies. Earle writes an English poem of 90 lines, in his memory (which was not printed until 1647. It is in Beaumont and Fletcher's *Comedies & Tragedies, &c.*, fol. and is headed *On Mr. Beavmont*, (written thirty yeares since, presently after his death.)
1616. — Sir T. Overbury's *Wife, now a Widdowe* published.
1619. July 8. 'John Earl of Merton Coll.' takes his B.A. *Wood. Fasti* æt. 18. *Oxon. Ed.* 1815.

Fellow of Merton College, Oxford. {
1620.* — He "was admitted probationers' fellow of Merton Coll. æt. 19. in 1620, aged 19 years or thereabouts, and proceeded in arts four years after. His younger years were adorned with oratory, poetry, and witty fancies; and his elder with quaint preaching and subtile disputes." *Wood. Ath. Oxon. idem.*
1624. July 10. He takes his M.A. *Dr. Bliss:* '*Micro-cosmography*,' æt. 23. *Ed.* 1811, *p.* 212.

1625. Mar. 27. Charles I ascends the throne.

1627. Aug. Sir J. Burroughs killed by a bullet at the Isle of Ré. æt. 26. Earle writes *Lines on Sir John Burroughs*, now in MS. in the Bodleian. *Reprinted by Dr. Bliss, idem. p.* 227.
1628. — Three first editions of *Micro-cosmographie* are published. Possibly also a fourth edition.
1630. Apr. 10. William Earl of Pembroke, Chancellor of the University, dies. Earle writes lines *On the death of the Earl of Pembroke*, in the same Bodleian MS., *Dr. Bliss, idem.*

A clerical disturbance occurs in the University. The King directs the two proctors to resign, and to be replaced by others of the same college. Earle succeeds J. Doughty of Merton. *Wood, Hist. & Ant. of Oxford,* ii. 372—380.

1631. Aug. 26. } 'Mr. John Ear of Merton coll. presented [as Proctor]
1632. Apr 10 } 26 Aug.' *Fasti Oxon. Ed.* 1815. He was 'about that time Chaplain to Philip, Earl of Pembroke' *Ath. Oxon. idem.*

1632. Is incorporated in Cambridge University.
Lord Clarendon, in his *Life,* thus writes ;

DOCTOR *Earles* was at that Time Chaplain in the House to the Earl of *Pembroke,* Lord Chamberlain of his Majesty's Houshold, and had a Lodging in the Court under that Relation : He was a Person very notable for his Elegance in the *Greek* and *Latin* Tongues ; and being Fellow of *Merton* College in *Oxford,* and having been Proctor of the University, and some very witty, and sharp Discourses being published in Print without his Consent, though known to be his, He grew suddenly into a very general Esteem with all Men ; being a Man of great Piety and Devotion ; a most eloquent and powerful Preacher; and of a Conversation so pleasant and delightful, so very innocent, and so very facetious, that no Man's Company was more desired, and more loved. No Man was more negligent in his Dress, and Habit, and Mien ; no Man more wary, and cultivated, in his Behaviour, and Discourse ; insomuch as He had the greater Advantage when He was known, by promising so little before He was known. He was an excellent Poet, both in *Latin, Greek,* and *English,* as appears by many Pieces yet abroad; though He suppressed many more himselfe, especially of *English,* incomparably good, out of an Austerity to those Sallies of his Youth. He was very dear to the Lord *Falkland,* with whom He spent as much Time as He could make his own ; and as that Lord would impute the speedy Progress He made in the *Greek* Tongue, to the Information and Assistance He had from Mr. *Earles,* so Mr. *Earles* would frequently profess, that He had got more useful Learning by his Conversation at *Tew* (the Lord *Falkland's* House) than He had at *Oxford.* In the first settling of the Prince his Family, He was made one of his Chaplains ; and attended on him when He was forced to leave the Kingdom. He was amongst the few excellent Men who never had, nor ever could have an Enemy, but such a one, who was an Enemy to all Learning, and Virtue, and therefore would never make himself known. i. 26. *Ed.* 1759.

'The famous Verses made upon *Merton* College Garden in *Oxford,* by Dr. *John Earl,* then a Fellow of that house,' were first printed in J. Aubrey, *Nat. Hist of Surrey,* iv. 166—171. *Ed.* 1716. The poem is in Latin, is entitled *Hortus Mertonensis,* and consists of 128 lines.

1639. æt. 38. Philip, Earl of Pembroke, presents him to the Rectory of Bishopston, in Wiltshire, and in the diocese of Salisbury. He was not finally released from the care of this parish until his elevation, in 1662, to the See of Worcester.
[*1664. æt. 63.] When, after this, he became bishop of his old diocese, he presented his former parish with its present existing communion plate. *Sir R. C. Hoare, History of Wilts,* ii. *Ed.* 1825.

1640. Nov. 10. 'John Earle sometimes fellow of Mert. coll. now chaplain to Charles prince of Wales,' is made Doctor of Divinity. *Wood. Fasti. Oxon. Ed.* 1820.

CHRONICLE. 5

1643. Feb. 10. He succeeds, on the death of the celebrated William æt. 42. Chillingworth, to the Chancellorship of Salisbury. *Wood. Ath. Oxon. iii.* 95, 717. *Ed.* 1817.

Elected one of the Assembly of Divines, but refuses to sit among them.

Afterwards he suffered, and was deprived of all he had, for adhering to his majesty King Charles I.

He was an intimate acquaintance with Dr. Morley, afterwards Bp. of Winchester, and lived with him one year at Antwerp, in Sir Charles Cotterell's house, who was master of the ceremonies. *Ath. Oxon. idem.*

*1645–51. [Dr. Smith writes to Hearne on 13 Sept. 1705. "Bp. Earle's Latin translation of Hooker's book of *Ecclesiastical Polity*, which was his entertainment, during part of his exile at Cologne, is utterly destroyed by prodigious heedlessness and carelessness: for it being written in loose papers, only pinned together, and put into a trunk unlocked, after his death, and being looked upon as refuse and waste paper, the servants lighted their fire with them, or else put them under their bread and their pies, as often as they had occasion; as the present earl of Clarendon has more than once told me, who was ordered by my lord his father, about a year after the bishop's death, to attend upon the widow, at her house near Salisbury, and to receive them from her hands, from whom he received this deplorable account of their loss; himself seeing several scattered pieces, not following in order, the number of pages being greatly interrupted, that had not undergone the same fate with the rest." *Orig. letter in Bodleian: see Ath. Oxon. iii.* 718. *note. Ed.* 1817.]

1647. Mar. 16. Lord Clarendon, then Sir E. Hyde, writing to Earle, combats some expressions of his, in a previous letter, 'I know not what you mean by the King's unnecessarily provoking them.' . . . . 'Is it possible that you can think (in this horrid alteration) the mere living in England with your friends, could restore you to the old delight and comfort in those friends you have formerly enjoyed, let all unjustifiable circumstances be out of the way:' Towards the end he says 'I would desire you (at your leisure) to send me that discourse of your own which you read to me at Dartmouth in the end of your contemplations upon the Proverbs, in memory of my Lord Falkland.' *Stat. Papers ii.* 348—350. *Ed.* 1773.

The Commonwealth.

1649. Is published Earle's translation into Latin of εἰκὼν βασιλική.

1651. 'He suffered in exile with his son king Charles II. whom, after his defeat at Worcester, he saluted at Rouen upon his arrival in Normandy, and thereupon was made his chaplain and clerk of the closet.' *Ath. Oxon. idem.*

1660. The Restoration.

1660. æt. 59. Earle returns to England. Is made Dean of Westminster.

"He beareth *Ermine*, on a Chief indented *Sable*, three Eastern Crowns *Or*, by the name of *Earles*. This Coat was granted by Sir *Edward Walker* Garter, the 1660. Aug. 1. 1st of *August* 1660, to the Reverend Dr *John Earles*, Son of *Tho. Earles* Gent. Sometime Register of the Arch-bishop's Court at *York*. He was Dean of *Westminster*, and Clerk of the Closet to his Majesty King

An exile on the Continent.

Dean of Westminster.

CHRONICLE.

Charles the Second, and in the Year 1663, made Bishop of *Salisbury.*" *J. Guillim. A Display of Heraldry.* Ed. 1724, *p*. 282.

Dn. of Westmnstr.
1661. Mar. 25. Is one of the commission to review the Prayer-Book. *Bp. Kennet's Reg. p.* 398. *Ed.* 1728.
28. (Good Friday.) As one of the Lenten preachers, preaches at Court. *Idem p.* 368.
Apr. 23. Assists at the King's coronation. *Idem p.* 417.
1662. June 20-23. Correspondence with Rev. R. Baxter. *Idem p.* 714.

Bishop.
1662. Nov. 30. Consecrated at Westminster Abbey, Bp. of Worcester: by the Bps. of London, Winchester, Salisbury, Chichester, Gloucester. *Idem p.* 823.
1663. æt. 62. Is translated to the see of Salisbury.

1665. The plague of London. The Court moves to Oxford and Bp. Earle goes with it. He 'took up his quarters in
Nov. 17. University college where dying on the 17 Novemb. 1665,
æt. 65. was buried near the high altar in Mert. coll. church, on
Nov. 25. the 25th day of the said month, being then accompanied to his grave from the public schools by an herald at arms and the principal persons of the court and university. *Ath. Oxon. idem.*

Death.
Bp. Burnet tells us "Doctor *Earl,* Bishop of *Salisbury,* died at that time. But, before his death, he declared himself much against this [the Five Mile] Act. He was the man of all the Clergy for whom the King had the greatest esteem. He had been his sub-tutor, and had followed him in all his exile with so clear a Character, that the King could never see or hear of any one thing amiss in him. So he, who had a secret pleasure in finding out any thing that lessened a man esteemed eminent for piety, yet had a value for him beyond all the men of his order." *History of my own times,* i. 225. *Ed.* 1724.

Dr. Calamy, a Nonconformist, adds similar testimony. "Dr. *Earle,* Bishop of Salisbury, was a Man that could do Good against Evil, forgive much out of a charitable Heart. He died to the no great Sorrow of them, who reckoned his death was just, for labouring all his Might against *the Oxford five Mile Act.*" *Abridgement,* i.

MICRO-COSMOGRAPHIE.

INTRODUCTION.

The Literature of Proteſtant England paſſed, about the time of James I., from the exuberant delicious fancifulneſs of youth into the ſober deliberativeneſs of manhood. The age of romantic chivalry, of daring diſcovery, of ſurpaſſing danger, was paſſing away. A time of wonderful thoughtfulneſs, of ſtrong reſearch, of national quiet had come. Learning had become common to moſt educated perſons. The moſt recondite ſubjects in theology and among the Schoolmen, the higheſt problems in nature, the ſubtleſt inquiries into the human ſpirit, the firſt principles of human ſociety, every theory of national government, daunted not, but faſcinated thinkers. Selden owned, 'All Confeſs there never was a more Learned Clergy, no Man taxes them with Ignorance'[*]; and the writings of Bacon, Lord Herbert of Cherbury, Hales, Selden, Hobbes, Prynne and others, repreſent the attainments of many of the laity.

The thinkers influenced the people. The words *Preciſian* and *Puritan*, creations of this epoch, teſtify to the growing ſeriouſneſs of the nation. In theſe earlier years of Puritaniſm eſpecially; and generally throughout the Seventeenth Century, there was a ſtrong paſſion for analyſis of human character. Men delighted in introſpection. Eſſays and Characters took the place of the Romances of the former century. Of them all, there is no complete liſt. Dr. Bliſs, to an edition of the preſent work, in 1811, added a liſt of

---

[*] *Table-Talk*, p. 37, Ed. 1868.

fifty-feven characters and books of characters: all—with one exception, in 1567—publifhed between 1605—1700. Forty-four years later, writing in 1855, to *Notes and Queries*,* he ftated that this lift 'in his own interleaved copy had increafed fourfold.'

Of all thefe *Micro-cofmographie* was one of the moft popular. Five editions apparently were publifhed in the firft two years of publication, and five more during the author's lifetime.

The authorfhip of the prefent work was never authoritatively announced. Univerfal confent, in his own time, attributed it to John Earle, then a Fellow of Merton College, Oxford. The firft fifty-four Characters, at leaft, may therefore be looked upon as the compofition 'efpecially for his private recreation, to pafs away the time in the country' of an Oxford man, not twenty-nine years of age, when they appeared in print; and which we are informed had previously circulated in manufcript, 'paffing from hand to hand in written Copies.'†

The writing of Characters was not a new thing when Earle penned the following ones. Not to mention minor works of this clafs, we may refer to Bifhop Hall's *Characters of Vertues and Vices* of 1608; and the Characters of Sir Thomas Overbury and his friends, attached to *A Wife, now a Widdowe*, firft publifhed in 1614.

The title given to the prefent work, is not the leaft apt thing in it. *Micro-cofmographie* means 'a defcription of the little world' (*i.e.*, man). Sir Walter Raleigh in his *Hiftorie of the World* firft publifhed in 1614, had thus referred to the old idea of man being a world within himfelf;

"The body of man (faith *Zanchius*) is the image of the world, and called therefore Microcofmus; Bk 1, Chap 2. § 1. p 20. . . .

* No. 299, 21st July, 1855. † p. 18.

.. Therefore (faith GREGORY NAZIANZENE,) *Homo eſt utriuſque naturæ vinculum, Man is the bond and chaine which tyeth together both natures:* and becauſe in the little frame of mans body there is a repreſentation of the Univerſal; and (by alluſion) a kinde of participation of all the parts there, therefore was man called *Micro-coſmos,* or the little World. *Deus igitur hominem factum, velut alterum quendam mundum, in brevi magnum, atque exiguo totum, in terris ſtatuit; God therefore placed in the Earth the man he had made, as it were another World; the great and large World in the ſmall and little World."* Bk. 1, Chap 2, § 5, p. 26.

Another Oxford man, Rev., afterwards Dr., Peter Heylin,—whoſe Epitaph was long after written by Earle, when Dean of Weſtminſter—had publiſhed at Oxford a geographical treatiſe, in 4to., entitled " Μικρόκοσμος A little deſcription of the Great World," of which three editions appeared in 1622, 1625, and 1627. Earle reverſes this title in this work, and gives us a 'deſcription of the little world' of man.

Eſſays deal rather with the permanent, internal, eſſential conſtituents; Characters with the paſſing, external, accidental aſpects of men. Of both there are examples in the preſent work. Some of the papers are delineations of human nature, common to all time ; others are inciſive deſcriptions of 'characters' and ſcenes of the writer's age, which have now paſſed away. Poſterity is as equally indebted to John Earle for his keen obſervations of human kind, as for his literary photographs of manners and life in England between, ſay the years 1618 and 1628.

BIBLIOGRAPHY.

INTRODUCTORY.

Confusion has arisen as to the actual number of essays in the several early editions of *Micro-Cosmographie*, through the somewhat careless editing Blount bestowed on their numbering and indexing. We have therefore constructed the following table of issues in the author's life time; from which it will be seen that the Characters first appeared in three several quantities, viz., fifty-four in 1628, twenty-three more in 1629, and one more in 1633. So that virtually the composition of these observations on English life and manners cannot be placed lower than 1629.

In the table, figures *without* the brackets ( ) are those printed at the head of the several Characters. The absence of any such figure is indicated by —; the omission of a Character altogether by *. These figures coincide with the actual order of the several essays, except when followed by others *within* ( ), which then represent the true order.

By the help of this table, the priority of the three editions of 1628 may be determined; the criterion being the carelessness of the editor.

Taking the *ostensible* figures *without* the brackets ( ), as on the pages 12—15,

   (1) a and b have no 8 or 29.

        misprint 50 for 51 : 52, 53, 54, 55, which should have followed as 53, 54, 55, 56.

      but a misprints 37 for 39, 47 for 49, which are corrected in b : shewing a partial correction.

     ∴ a is anterior to b.

   c   assigns 8 and 29 to characters.
        has no misprints in the *ostensible* figures.
        rearranges the numbers generally.

     ∴ c is a correction of b.

   (2) *The Herald* is omitted the in index of a, but is inserted in those of b and c.

The title-page of a is reprinted at page 17, and those of b and c on the opposite page.

The text of the present edition is, for the first fifty-four essays, that of a of 1628, collated with b and c of that year; for next twenty-three, the fifth edition, 1629; and for the last one, that of 1633; in which editions they first appear.

BIBLIOGRAPHY. 11

TITLE-PAGES
[reduced]
of
Second and Third Editions
of
1628.

b

Micro-cosmographie.
OR,
A PEECE OF
THE WORLD
DISCOVERED;
IN ESSAYES AND
CHARACTERS.

LONDON,
Printed by *William Stansby* for
Robert Allot. 1628.

c

Micro-cosmographie.
OR,
A PEECE OF
THE WORLD
DISCOVERED;
IN ESSAYES AND
CHARACTERS.

*Newly Composed for the Northerne
parts of this Kingdome.*

AT LONDON,
Printed by W. S. for *Ed: Blount,*
1628.

(a) Issues in the Author's life time.

CHARACTERS.	1628 a *William Stansby for Edward Blount.* [? Editio princeps.]	1628 b *William Stansby for R. Allot.*	1628 c *W.S. for Ed. Blount.*	1629. *The Fifth Edition.* [? 4th Ed. 1628 or 1629]	1630. *The Sixth Edition augmented.*	1633. *The Sixth Edition augmented.*	1638. *The Seventh Edition augmented.*	1642. *description of the Pot-companion Poet: who* *abroad. Also, Characters of the Suit-bolt Cook.* *any other trace of this edition.*	1650. *W. Bentley for William Shears.*	1664. *The Eighth Edition.*
Actual order in the first edition.										
1. A child.	1	1	1	1		1	1		1	1
2. A young raw preacher.	2	2	2	2		2	2		2	2
3. A grave divine.	3	3	3	3	(5)	3	3		3	3
4. A mere dull phyfician.	4	4	4	—	(7)	—	5		4	5
5. An alderman.	5	5	5	6	(8)	7	7		5	7
6. A difcontented man.	6	6	6	7	(9)	8	8		6	8
7. An antiquary.	7	7	7	8		9	9		7	9
8. A younger brother.	9 (8)	9 (8)	9	10(11)		11	11		8	11
9. A formal man.	10 (9)	10 (9)	10	11(12)		12	12		9	12
10. A church-Papift.	11(10)	11(10)	11	11(13)		13	13		10	13
11. A felf-conceited man.	12(11)	12(11)	12	13(15)		15	15		11	15
12. A tavern.	13(12)	13(12)	13	16(18)		18	18		12	18
13. A referved man.	14(13)	14(13)	14	15(17)		17	17		13	17
14. A fhark.	15(14)	15(14)	15	—(19)		19	19		14	19
15. A carrier.	16(15)	16(15)	16	22		22	22		15	22

No eighth.

BIBLIOGRAPHY.

16.	An old College butler.	17(16)	17(16)	17	26	26	26	16	26
17.	An upftart knight.	18(17)	18(17)	18	28	28	28	17	28
18.	An idle gallant.	19(18)	19(18)	19	30	30	30	18	30
19.	A conftable.	20(19)	20(19)	20	31	31	31	19	31
20.	A down-right fcholar.	21(20)	21(20)	25	33	33	33	20	33
21.	A player.	22(21)	22(21)	24	38	38	38	21	38
22.	A detractor.	23(22)	23(22)	26	39	39	39	22	39
23.	A young gentleman of the Univerfity.	24(23)	24(23)	23	41	41	41	24(23)	41
24.	A pot poet.	25(24)	25(24)	27	45	45	45	24	45
25.	A cook.	26(25)	26(25)	22	63	63	63	25	63
26.	A forward man.	27(26)	27(26)	29	64	64	64	26	64
27.	A baker.	28(27)	28(27)	21	65	65	65	27	65
28.	A plain country fellow.	30(28)	30(28)	28	35	35	35	28	35
29.	A young man.	31(29)	31(29)	30	—(25)	25	25	29	25
30.	The common finging-men.	32(30)	32(30)	31	69	69	69	30	69
31.	A pretender to learning.	33(31)	33(31)	32	66	66	66	31	66
32.	A fhopkeeper.	34(32)	34(32)	33	70	70	70	32	70
33.	A handfome hoftefs.	35(33)	35(33)	34	72	72	72	33	72
34.	A blunt man.	36(34)	36(34)	34(35)	71	71	71	34	71
35.	A critic.	37(35)	37(35)	35(36)	73	73	73	35	73
36.	A ferjeant.	38(36)	38(36)	36(37)	73(74)	74	74	35(36)	74
37.	A weak man.	37	39(37)	37(38)	42	42	42	37	42
38.	A tobacco feller.	40(38)	40(38)	39	43	43	43	38	43
39.	A plaufible man.	41(39)	41(39)	38(40)	46	46	46	39	46
40.	The worldlywife man.	42(40)	42(40)	40(41)	48	48	48	41(40)	48

No twenty-nine. (row 29) *No copy known: neither is there* Characters 24 and 25, printed separately in 4to., under the title of *A true is the Founder of all the Bafe and Libellous Pamphlets lately spread*.

(a) Issues in the Author's life time.

CHARACTERS.	1628. a William Stansby for Edward Blount. [? Editio princeps.]	1628. b William Stansby for R. Allot.	1628. c W. S. for Ed. Blount.	1629. The Fifth Edition. (4th Ed. 1628 & 1629, other trace of this edition.)	1630. The Sixth Edition augmented.	1633. The Sixth Edition augmented.	1638. The Seventh Edition augmented. (1642. description of the Pot-companion Poet; abroad. Also, Character of the Suit.)	1650. W. Bentley for William Shears.	1644. The Eighth Edition.
Actual order in the first edition.									
41. A bowling-alley.	43(41)	43(41)	41(42)	47		47	47	42(41)	47
42. A surgeon.	44(42)	44(42)	42(43)	49		49	49	43(42)	49
43. A she-precise hypocrite.	45(43)	45(43)	43(44)	52		52	52	44(43)	52
44. A contemplative man.	46(44)	46(44)	44(45)	51		51	51	45(44)	51
45. An attorney.	47(45)	47(45)	8	54		54	54	46(45)	54
46. A sceptic in religion.	48(46)	48(46)	46(47)	53		53	53	47(46)	53
47. A partial man.	47	49(47)	47(48)	56		56	56	49(47)	56
48. A trumpeter.	50(48)	50(48)	49	57		57	57	49(48)	57
49. A vulgar-spirited man.	50(49)	50(49)	49(50)	58		53	58	50(49)	58
50. A herald.	52(50)	52(50)	43(51)	68		68	68	51(50)	96(68)
51. A plodding Student.	52(51)	52(51)	51(52)	49(59)		59	59	52(51)	59
52. Paul's walk.	53(52)	53(52)	52(53)	61		61	61	52	61
53. An University dun.	54(53)	54(53)	45(46)	76		76	76	53	76
54. A staid man.	55(54)	55(54)	52(54)	77		77	77	54	77

BIBLIOGRAPHY.

Present Order.	Additional Characters in Fifth Edition.				
55.	A modest man.	4	4	4	55
56.	A mere empty wit.	(6)	6	6	57(56)
57.	A drunkard.	—	10	10	58(57)
58.	A prison.	9(10)	14	14	60(58)
59.	A servingman.	—	16	16	61(59)
60.	An infolent man.	(14)	20	20	62(60)
61.	Acquaintance.	14(16)	21	21	63(61)
62.	A mere complemental man.	20	23	23	64(62)
63.	A poor fidler.	21	24	24	65(63)
64.	A medling man.	23	27	27	67(65)
65.	A good old man.	24	29	29	66(64)
66.	A flatterer.	27	32	32	68(66)
67.	A high spirited man.	29	34	34	69(67)
68.	A mere gull citizen.	32	36	36	*
69.	A lascivious man.	34	37	37	70(68)
70.	A rash man.	36	40	40	71(69)
71.	An affected man.	37	44	44	*
72.	A profane man.	40	50	50	72(70)
73.	A coward.	44	55	55	73(71)
74.	A sordid rich man.	50	60	60	74(72)
75.	A mere great man.	55	62	62	76(73)
76.	A poor nun.	60	67	67	*
77.	An ordinary honest fellow.	62	75	75	77(74)
	Additional Character in Sixth Edition (1633).	67			
		75			
78.	A suspicious or jealous man.	*	78	78	*

No copy known: neither is there any

Characters 24 and 25, printed separately in 4to., under the title of *A true who is the Founder of all the Base and Lewd Pamphlets lately spread bolt Cook*.

BIBLIOGRAPHY.

† Editions not seen.
b. Issues since the Author's Death.

I. As a separate work.

12. 1669. London. *Micro-cofmographie*, &c. *The Ninth Edition*,
1 vol. 12mo. (78 characters).

14. † 1676. Lond. 'The remaining copies of the ninth
1 vol. 12mo. (1669) edition, with a different title.' *Dr. Blifs, in Notes and Queries, No.* 299.

? † 1677. London. 'Seventy eight characters of fo many vertu-
1 vol. 8vo. ous and vitious perfons; written by one well acquainted with moft of them.' *W. C. Hazlitt's Handbook*, p. 84. ed. 1867. [? Can this be another edition.]

15. † 1732. Lond. Microcofmography, 'a reprint from the
* 1 vol. 8vo. fixth edition of 1633.' *Dr. Bliss, idem.*

16. 1740. London. The World difplay'd: or Several Effays;
1 vol. 8vo. confifting of the various Characters and paffions of its principal Inhabitants. (78 Characters: the laft eight are wrongly numbered 72—79).

18. † 1786. Salis- Microcofmography. 'This profeffes to be
bury. 1 vol. 8vo. taken from the edition of 1650, and is of courfe incomplete.' *Dr. Bliss, idem.* It was reprinted by William Benfon Earle, mufician: fee *Hatcher's, Sarum ii.* 651; *in Sir R. C. Hoare's Hiftory of Modern Wiltfhire.*

19. 1811. London. Microcofmography. Ed. by Dr. P. BLISS.
1 vol. 8vo. The text is that of 1732 [which is again a reprint of 1633] collated with an edition of 1628.
25 July 1855. Dr. Bliss writes to *Notes and Queries*, 'The book is too common [?] and unimportant [?] to induce any publifher to venture on fuch an undertaking' [as republifhing it].

22. 1 Dec. 1868. *Englifh Reprints:* fee title at p. 1. A col-
Lond. 1 vol. 8vo. lation of the five earlieft extant editions; see p. 10.

II. With other works.

17. 1742. London. The World Difplay'd: or, Mankind painted
1 vol. 8vo. . in their proper Colours [A numerous collection of characters, including many by Earle. Quite a different work from 15.]

21. 1865. Edin- 'A Book of Characters: felected from the
burgh. 1 vol. 8vo. writings of Overbury, Earle, and Butler. (Includes 68 Characters by Earle.)

III. Adaptations, tranflations, &c.

13. † 1671. London. Into French by J. Dymock. *Le Vice ridi-*
1 vol. 8vo. *culé et la Vertue Louée. Hazlitt, Handbook.*

20. 1813. Dublin. A Gallery of Portraits, painted by an old and
1 vol. 8vo. celebrated Mafter, and re-touched by an Irifh artift.

Micro-cosmographie,

OR,

A PEECE OF THE WORLD DISCOVERED;

IN ESSAYES AND CHARACTERS.

LONDON,
Printed by *William Stansby* for
Edward Blount, 1628.

TO
THE READER
GENTILE OR
GENTLE.

Haue (for once) aduentur'd to playe the Mid-wifes part, helping to bring forth thefe Infants into the World, which the Father would haue fmoothered: who hauing left them lapt vp in loofe Sheets, as foon as his Fancy was deliuered of them; written especially for his priuate Recreation, to paffe away the time in the Country, and by the forcible requeſt of Friends drawne from him; Yet paffing feuerally from hand to hand in written Copies, grew at length to be a prety number in a little Volume: and among fo many fundry difperfed Tranfcripts, fome very imperfect and furreptitious had like to haue paſt the Preffe, if the Author had not vfed fpeedy meanes of preuention: When, perceiuing the hazard hee ran to be wrong'd, was vnwillingly willing to let them paffe as now they appear to the World. If any faults haue efcap'd the Preffe, (as few Bookes can bee printed without) impofe them not on the Author I intreat Thee; but rather impute them to mine and the Printers ouerfight, who ferioufly promife on the re impreffion hereof by greater care and diligence, for this our former default, to make Thee ample fatisfaction. In the meanwhile, I remaine
Thine.

ED. BLOVNT.

A TABLE OF CONTENTS.

[In firſt edition of 1628 only: which edition has no pagination. The figures are the numbers of the Characters, and have been corrected to the true figures, as explained at p. 10.]

A Childe.	1.
A young raw Preacher.	2.
A graue Diuine.	3.
A meere dull Phyſitian.	4.
An Alderman.	5.
A diſcontented Man.	6.
An Antiquary.	7.
A younger Brother.	8.
A formall Man.	9.
A Church-Papiſt.	10.
A ſelfe-conceited man.	11.
A Tauerne.	12.
A reſeru'd Man.	13.
A Sharke.	14.
A Carier.	15.
An old Colledge Butler.	16.
An Vpſtart Knight.	17.
An idle Gallant.	18.
A Conſtable.	19.
A downe-right Scholler.	20.
A Player.	21.
A Detractor.	22.
A young Gentleman of the Vniuerſity.	23.

The Table.

A Pot-Poet.	24.
A Cooke.	25.
A forward Man.	26.
A Baker.	27.
A plaine Country Fellow.	28.
A Young-Man.	29.
The common Singing-Men.	30.
A Pretender to Learning.	31.
A Shop keeper.	32.
A Handsome Hostesse.	33.
A blunt Man.	34.
A Criticke.	35.
A Sergeant.	36.
A weake Man.	37.
A Tobacco seller.	38.
A plausible Man.	39.
The Worlds wise Man.	40.
A Bowle-Alley.	41.
A Surgeon.	42.
A Shee-precise Hypocrite.	43.
A Contemplatiue Man.	44.
An Aturney.	45.
A Sceptick in religion.	46.
A Partiall man.	47.
A Trumpeter.	48.
A vulgar-spirited Man.	49.
[*A Herald*	50.]
A plodding Student.	51.
Pauls Walke.	52.
An Vniuersity Dun.	53.
A stayed Man.	54.

FINIS.

* The omission of this character in the table has been the cause of much confusion.

Micro-cosmographie.
OR,
A piece of the World Characteriz'd.

1. *A Childe*

AS a Man in a small Letter, yet the best Copie of *Adam* before hee tasted of *Eue*, or the Apple; and hee is happy whose small practice in the World can only write this Character. Hee is natures fresh picture newly drawn in Oyle, which time and much handling, dimmes and defaces. His Soule is yet a white paper vnscribled with obseruations of the world, wherewith at length it becomes a blurr'd Note-booke. He is purely happy, because he knowes no euill, nor hath made meanes by sinne to bee acquainted with misery. Hee arriues not at the mischiefe of being wise, nor endures euils to come by foreseeing them. He kisses and loues all, and when the smart of the rod is past, smiles on his beater. Nature and his Parents alike dandle him, and tice him on with a bait of Sugar, to a draught of Worme wood. He playes yet, like a young Prentise the first day, and is not come to his taske of melancholly. His hardest labour is his tongue, as if he were loath to vse so deceitfull an Organ; and hee

is beft company with it when hee can but prattle. Wee
laugh at his foolifh fports, but his game is our earneft:
and his drummes, rattles and hobby-horfes, but the
Emblems, and mocking of mans bufineffe. His father
hath writ him as his owne little ftory, wherein hee
reades thofe dayes of his life that hee cannot remember; and fighes to fee what innocence he has out liu'd.
The elder he growes, hee is a ftayer lower from God;
and like his firft father much worfe in his breeches.
He is the Chriftians example, and the old mans re-
lapfe: The one imitates his pureneffe, and the other
fals into his fimplicitie. Could hee put off his body
with his little Coate, he had got eternitie without a
burthen, and exchang'd but one Heauen for another.

2. *A young rawe Preacher*

IS a Bird not yet fledg'd, that hath hopt out
of his neft to bee Chirping on a hedge,
and will bee ftragling abroad at what perill
foeuer. His backwardneffe in the Vni-
uerfitie hath fet him thus forward; for had
thee not ruanted there, he had not beene fo haftie
a Diuine. His fmall ftanding and time hath made
him a proficient onely in boldneffe, out of which and
his Table booke he is furnifht for a Preacher. His
Collections of Studie are the notes of Sermons, which
taken vp at St. *Maries*, hee vtters in the Country. And
if he write brachigraphy, his ftocke is fo much the
better. His writing is more then his reading; for hee
reades onely what hee gets without booke. Thus ac-
complifht he comes down to his friends, and his firft
falutation is grace and peace out of the Pulpit. His
prayer is conceited, and no man remembers his Colledge more at large. The pace of his Sermon is a ful
careere, and he runnes wildly ouer hill and dale till the
clocke ftop him. The labour of it is chiefly in his
lungs. And the onely thing hee ha's made of it himfelfe, is the faces. He takes on againft the Pope

without mercy, and ha's a ieſt ſtill in lauender for *Bellarmine.* Yet he preaches hereſie, if it comes in his way, though with a mind I muſt needs ſay very Orthodoxe. His action is all paſſion, and his ſpeech interiections: He ha's an excellent faculty in bemoaning the people, and ſpits with a very good grace. His ſtile is compounded of ſome twenty ſeueral mens, onely his body imitates ſome one extraordinary. He wil not draw his handkercher out of his place, nor blow his noſe without diſcretion. His commendation is, that he neuer looks vpon booke, and indeed, he was neuer vs'd to it. Hee preaches but once a yeare, though twice on Sund[a]y: for the ſtuffe is ſtill the ſame, onely the dreſſing a little alter'd. He has more tricks with a ſermon, then a Tailer with an old cloak, to turne it, and piece it, and at laſt quite diſguiſe it with a new preface. If he haue waded further in his profeſſion, and would ſhew reading of his own, his Authors are Poſtils, and his Schoole-diuinitie a Catechiſme. His faſhion and demure Habit gets him in with ſome Town-preciſian and maks him a Gueſt on Fryday nights. You ſhall know him by his narrow Veluet cape, and Serge facing, and his ruffe, next his haire, the ſhorteſt thing about him. The companion of his walke is ſome zealous tradeſman, whom he aſtoniſheth with ſtrange points, which they both vnderſtand alike. His friends and much painefulneſſe may preferre him to thirtie pounds a yeere, and this means, to a chambermaide: with whom wee leaue him now in the bonds of Wedlocke. Next Sunday you ſhal haue him againe.

3. *A Graue Diuine*

IS one that knowes the burden of his calling, and hath ſtudied to make his ſhoulders ſufficient: for which hee hath not beene haſty to launch foorth of his port the Vniuerſitie, but expected the ballaſt of learning, and the winde of opportunitie. Diuinitie is not the beginning but the end of his ſtudies, to which hee takes the ordinary ſtayre, and makes the Arts his way. Hee counts it not profaneneſſe to bee poliſht with humane reading, or to ſmooth his way by *Ariſtotle* to Schoole-diuinitie. He ha's founded both Religions and anchord in the beſt, and is a Proteſtant out of iudgement, not faction, not becauſe his Country, but his Reaſon is on this ſide. The miniſtry is his choyce, not refuge, and yet the Pulpit not his itch, but feare. His diſcourſe there is ſubſtance, not all Rhetorique, and he vtters more things then words. His ſpeech is not help't with enforc'd action, but the matter acts it ſelfe. Hee ſhoots all his meditations at one Butt: and beats vpon his Text, not the Cuſhion, making his hearers not the Pulpit groane. In citing of Popiſh errors, he cuts them with Arguments, not cudgels them with barren inuectiues: and labours more to ſhew the truth of his cauſe then the ſpleene. His Sermon is limited by the method, not the houre-glaſſe.; and his Deuotion goes along with him out of the Pulpit. He comes not vp thrice a weeke becauſe he would not be idle, nor talkes three houres together, becauſe he would not talke nothing: but his tongue Preaches at fit times, and his conuerſation is the euery dayes exerciſe. In matters of ceremonie hee is not ceremonious, but thinkes hee owes that reuerence to the Church to bow his iudgement to it, and make more conſcience of ſchiſme, then a Surpleſſe. Hee eſteemes the Churches Hirarchie, as the Churches glory, and how-euer wee iarre with Rome, would not haue our confuſion diſtinguiſh vs. In Symoniacall purchaſes he thinks his Soule goes in the bargaine, and is loath to come by promotion ſo deare. Yet his worth at the length aduances him, and the price of his owne merit buyes him a Liuing. He is no baſe Grater of his Tythes, and will not wrangle for the odde Egge. The Lawyer is the onely man he hinders, he is ſpited for taking vp quarrels. He is a maine pillar of our church, though not yet Deane nor Canon, and his life our Religions beſt Apologie: His death is his laſt Sermon, where in the Pulpit of his Bed hee inſtructs men to dye by his example.

4. *A meere dull Phiſitian.*

HIS practice is ſome buſineſſe at bed-ſides, and his ſpeculation an Vrinall. Hee is diſtinguiſht from an Empericke by a round veluet cap, and Doctors gowne, yet no man takes degrees more ſuperfluouſly, for he is Doctor howſoeuer. He is ſworne to *Galen* and *Hypocrates*, as Vniuerſity men to their ſtatues, though they neuer ſaw them, and his diſcourſe is all Aphoriſmes, though his reading be onely *Alexis* of Piemont, or the Regiment of Health. The beſt Cure he ha's done is vpon his own purſe, which from a leane ſickllineſſe he hath made luſty, and in fleſh. His learning conſiſts much in reckoning vp the hard names of diſeaſes, and the ſuperſcriptions of Gallypots in his Apothecaries Shoppe, which are rank't in his Shelues, and the Doctors memory. He is indeed only languag'd in diſeaſes, and ſpeakes Greeke many times when he knows not. If he haue beene but a by-ſtander at ſome deſperate recouery, he is ſlandered with it, though he be guiltleſſe; and this breeds his reputation, and that his Practice; for his skill is meerly opinion. Of al odors he likes beſt the ſmel of Vrine, and holds *Veſpatians* rule, that no gaine is vnſauory. If you ſend this once to him, you muſt reſolue to be ſicke howſoeuer, for he will neuer leaue examining your Water till hee haue ſhakt it into a diſeaſe. Then followes a writ to his drugger in a ſtrange tongue, which hee vnderſtands though he cannot conſter. If he ſee you himſelfe, his preſence is the worſt viſitation: for if he cannot heale your ſickneſs, he will bee ſure to helpe it. Hee tranſlates his Apothecaries Shop into your Chamber, and the very Windowes and benches muſt take Phiſicke. He tels you your Maladie in Greeke, though it be but a cold, or head ach: which

c

by good endeauour and diligence he may bring to some
moment indeed; his moſt vnfaithfull act is, that hee
leaues a man gaſping, and his pretence is, death and
he haue a quarrell, and muſt not meet; but his feare
is, leaſt the Carcaſſe ſhould bleed. Anotomies and
other ſpectacles of Mortalitie haue hardened him, and
hee's no more ſtruck with a Funerall then a Graue-
maker. Noblemen vſe him for a director of their
ſtomacks, and Ladies for wantonneſſe, eſpecially if hee
bee a proper man. If he be ſingle, he is in league
with his Shee-Apothecary, and becauſe it is the Phyſi-
tian, the huſband is Patient. If he haue leaſure to
be idle (that is to ſtudy) he ha's a ſmatch at Alcumy,
and is ſicke of the Philoſophers ſtone, a diſeaſe vn-
curable, but by an abundant Phlebotomy of the purſe.
His two maine oppoſites are a Mountebanke and a
good Woman, and hee neuer ſhewes his learning ſo
much as in an inuectiue againſt them, and their boxes.
In concluſion he is a ſucking conſumption, and a very
brother to the wormes, for they are both ingendred
out of mans corruption.

5. *An Alderman.*

Hee is Venerable in his Gowne, more in
his Beard, wherewith hee ſets not foorth
ſo much his owne, as the face of a Citie.
You muſt looke on him as one of the
Towne-gates, and conſider him not as a
Body, but a Corporation. His eminencie aboue others
hath made him a man of Worſhip, for hee had neuer
beene prefer'd, but that hee was worth thouſands. Hee
ouer-ſees the Common-wealth, as his Shop, and it
is an argument of his Policie, that he has thriuen by his
craft. Hee is a rigorous Magiſtrate in his Ward: yet
his ſcale of Iuſtice is ſuſpected, leaſt it bee like the
Ballances in his Ware-houſe. A ponderous man he is,
and ſubſtantiall: for his weight is commonly extraor-
dinarie, and in his preferment nothing riſes ſo much

as his Bellie. His head is of no great depth, yet well
furnisht, when it is in coniunction with his Brethren,
may bring foorth a Citie Apothegme, or some such sage
matter. Hee is one that will not haftily runne into
error, for hee treds with great deliberation, and his
iudgment confifts much in his pace. His difcourfe
is commonly the Annals of his Maioralty, and what
good gouerment there was in the dayes of his gold
Chaine: though his doore-pofts were the onely things
that fuffered reformation: Hee feemes not fincerely
religious, efpecially on folemne daies; for he comes
oft to Church to make a fhew. Hee is the higheft
ftayre of his profeffion, and an example to his Trade,
what in time they may come to. Hee makes very
much of his authority; but more of his Satin Doublet;
which though of good yeares, bears its age very well,
and looks frefh euery Sunday; But his Scarlet gowne
is a Monument, and lafts from generation to generation.

6. *A difcontented Man*

IS one that is falne out with the world, and
will bee reuenged on himfelfe. Fortune
ha's deny'd him in fomething, and hee
now takes pet, and will bee miferable in
fpite. The roote of his difeafe is a felfe-
humouring pride, and an accuftom'd tendernefse, not
to bee croft in his fancy: and the occafions commonly
one of thefe three, a hard Father, a peeuifh Wench, or
his ambition thwarted. Hee confidered not the nature
of the world till he felt it, and all blowes fall on him
heauier, becaufe they light not firft on his expectation.
Hee has now forgone all but his pride, and is yet vain
glorious in the oftentation of his melancholy. His
compofure of himfelf is a ftudied carelefneffe with his
armes a croffe, and a neglected hanging of his head
and cloake, and he is as great an enemie to an hat-
band, as Fortune. He quarrels at the time, and vp-
ftarts, and fighs at the neglect of men of Parts, that

is, such as himselfe. His life is a perpetuall Satyre, and
hee is still girding the ages vanity; when this very
anger shewes he too much esteemes it. Hee is much
displeas'd to see men merry, and wonders what they
can finde to laugh at. He neuer draws his own lips
higher then a smile, and frownes wrinckle him before
fortie. He at the last fals into that deadly melancholy
to bee a bitter hater of men, and is the most apt Companion for any mischiefe. Hee is the sparke that
kindles the Commonwealth, and the bellowes himselfe
to blow it: and if he turne any thing, it is commonly
one of these, either Friar, traitor, or mad-man.

7. *An Antiquary.*

Hee is a man strangely thrifty of Time past,
and an enemy indeed to his Maw, whence
he fetches out many things when they are
now all rotten and stinking. Hee is one
that hath that vnnaturall disease to bee
enamour'd of old age, and wrinckles, and loues
all things (as Dutchmen doe Cheese) the better for
being mouldy and worme-eaten. He is of our Religion, because wee say it is most ancient; and yet a
broken Statue would almost make him an Idolater. A
great admirer he is of the rust of old Monuments, and
reades onely those Charaƈters, where time hath eaten
out the letters. Hee will goe you forty miles to see a
Saints Well, or ruin'd Abbey: and if there be but a
Crosse or stone foot-stoole in the way, hee'l be considering it so long, till he forget his iourney. His
estate consists much in shekels, and Roman Coynes,
and hee hath more Piƈtures of Cæsar, then *Iames* or
Elizabeth. Beggers coozen him with musty things
which they haue rak't from dunghils, and he preserues
their rags for precious Reliques. He loues no
Library, but where there are more Spiders volums then
Authors, and lookes with great admiration on the
Antique worke of Cob-webs. Printed bookes he con-

temnes, as a nouelty of this latter age; but a Manufcript he pores on euerlaftingly, efpecially if the couer be all Moth-eaten, and the duft make a Parenthefis betweene euery Syllable. He would giue all the Bookes in his Study (which are rarities all) for one of the old Romane binding. or fixe lines of *Tully* in his owne hand. His chamber is hung commonly with ftrange Beafts fkins, and is a kind of Charnel-houfe of bones extraordinary and his difcourfe vpon them, if you will heare him fhall laft longer. His very atyre is that which is the eldeft out of fafhion, and you may picke a Criticifm out of his Breeches. He neuer lookes vpon himfelf till he is gray hair'd, and then he is pleafed with his owne Antiquity. His Graue do's not fright him, for he ha's been vs'd to Sepulchers, and hee likes Death the better, becaufe it gathers him to his Fathers.

8. *Younger Brother.*

His elder Brother was the *Efau*, that came out firft and left him like *Iacob* at his heeles. His father ha's done with him, as *Pharaoh* to the children of Ifrael, that would haue them make brick, and giue them no ftraw, fo he taskes him to bee a Gentleman, and leaues him nothing to maintaine it. The pride of his houfe has vndone him, which the elder Knighthood muft fuftaine, and his beggery that Knighthood. His birth and bringing vp will not fuffer him to defcend to the meanes to get wealth: but hee ftands at the mercy of the World, and which is worfe of his brother. He is fomething better then the Seruingmen; yet they more faucy with him, then hee bold with the mafter, who beholds him with a countenance of fterne awe, and checks him oftner then his Liueries. His brothers old fuites and hee are much alike in requeft, and caft off now and then one to the other. Nature hath furnifht him with a little more wit vpon

compaffion; for it is like to be his beft reuenew. If his
Annuity ftretch fo farre he is fent to the Vniuerfity, and
with great heart burning takes vpon him the Miniftry;
as a profeffion hee is condemn'd, to buy his ill fortune.
Other take a more crooked path, yet the Kings high
way, where at length their vizzard is pluck't off, and
they ftrike faire for Tiburne: but their Brothers pride,
not loue, gets them a pardon. His laft refuge is the
Low-counties, where rags and lice are no fcandall,
where he liues a poore Gentleman of a Company, and
dies without a fhirt. The onely thing that may better
his fortunes, is an art hee ha's to make a Gentlewoman,
wherewith hee baits now and then fome rich widow,
that is hungry after his blood. Hee is commonly dif-
contented, and defperate, and the forme of his excla-
mation is, that Churle my brother. Hee loues not
his country for this vnnatural cuftome, and would haue
long fince reuolted to the Spaniard, but for Kent onely
which he holds in admiration.

9. *A meere formall Man*

IS fomewhat more then the fhape of a man;
for he has his length, breadth, and colour.
When you haue feene his outfide, you
haue lookt through him, and need imploy your difcouery no farther. His reafon is meerly example, and his action is not guided
by his vnderftanding, but he fees other men doe thus,
and he followes them. He is a Negatiue, for we cannot call him a wife man, but not a foole; nor an honeft
man, but not a knaue; nor a Proteftant, but not a
Papift. The chiefe burden of his braine is the carriage of his body and the fetting of his face in a good
frame: which hee performes the better, becaufe hee
is not difioynted with other Meditations. His Religion is a good quiet fubiect, and he prayes as he
fweares, in the Phrafe of the Land. He is a faire gueft,
and a faire inuiter, and can excufe his good cheere in

the accustomed Apologie. Hee ha's some faculty in mangling of a Rabbet, and the distribution of his morsell to a neighbour trencher. Hee apprehends a iest by seeing men smile, and laughes orderly himselfe, when it comes to his turne. His discourse is the newes that hee hath gathered in his walke, and for other matters his discretion is, that he will onely what he can, that is, say nothing. His life is like one that runnes to the Minster walke, to take a turne, or two, and so passes. He hath staid in the world to fill a number; and when he is gone, there wants one, and there's an end.

10. *A Church-Papist*

IS one that parts his Religion betwixt his conscience and his purse, and comes to Church not to serue God, but the King. The face of the Law makes him weare the maske of the Gospel, which he vses not as a meanes to saue his soule, but charges. He loues Popery well, but is loath to lose by it, and though he be something scar'd with the Buls of Rome, yet they are farre off, and he is strucke with more terrour at the Apparitor. Once a moneth he presents himselfe at the Church, to keepe off the Church-warden, and brings in his body to saue his bayle. Hee kneels with the Congregation, but prayes by himselfe, and askes God forgiuenesse for comming thither. If he be forc'd to stay out a Sermon, he puts his hat ouer his eyes, and frowns out the houre, and when hee comes home, thinkes to make amends for this fault by abusing the Preacher. His maine policy is to shift off the Communion, for which he is neuer vnfurnish't of a quarrell, and will bee sure to be out of Charity at Easter; and indeed lies not, for hee ha's a quarrell to the Sacrament. He would make a bad Martyr, and good trauellor, for his conscience is so large, he could neuer wander out of it, and in Constantinople would bee circumcis'd with a referuation. His wife is more zealous, and therfore more coftly, and he bates her in tyres, what fhe ftands him in Religion. But we leaue him hatching plots againft the State, and expecting *Spinola*.

11. *A felfe-conceited Man*

IS one that knowes himfelfe fo well that he does not know himfelfe. Two excellent well-dones haue vndone him; and hee is guilty, that firft commended him to madneffe. He is now become to his own booke, which he poares on continually, yet like a truant-reader skips ouer the harfh places and furueyes onely that which is pleafant. In the fpeculation of his owne good parts, his eyes like a drunkards fee all double, and his fancy like an old mans fpectacles, make a great letter in a fmall print. He imagines euery place where hee comes his Theater, and not a looke ftirring, but his fpectator; and conceiues mens thoughts to bee very idle, that is, bufie about him. His walke is ftill in the fafhion of a March, and like his opinion vnaccompanyed, with his eyes moft fixt vpon his owne perfon, or on others with reflection to himfelfe. If hee haue done any thing that ha's paft with applaufe, he is alwayes re-acting it alone, and conceits the extafie his hearers were in at euery period. His difcourfe is all pofitions, and definitiue decrees, with thus it muft be, and thus it is, and he will not humble his authority to proue it. His tenent is always fingular, and aloofe from the vulgar as hee can, from which you muft not hope to wreft him. He ha's an excellent humor, for an Heretique, and in thefe days made the firft Arminian. He prefers *Ramus* before *Ariftotle*, and *Paracelfus* before *Galen*, and whofoeuer with moft Paradox is commended and *Lipfius* his hopping ftile, before either *Tully* or *Quintilian*. He much pitties the World, that ha's no more infight in his Parts, when he is too well difcouered, euen to this very tho[u]ght. A

flatterer is a dunce to him, for he can tell him nothing
but what hee knowes before, and yet he loues him to,
becaufe he is like himfelfe. Men are mercifull to him,
and let him alone, for if he be once driuen from his
humor, he is like two inward friends fallen out; His
own bitter enemy, and difcontent prefently makes a
murther. In fumme, he is a bladder blown vp with
wind, which the leaft flaw crufhes to nothing.

12. *A Tauerne*

IS a degree, or (if you will) a paire of ftayres
aboue an Alehoufe, where men are drunke
with more credit and Apologie. If the
Vintners nofe be at the doore, it is a
figne fufficient, but the abfence of this is
fupplyed by the Iuie bufh. The rooms are il breath'd,
like the drinkers that haue bin wafht well ouer night,
and are fmelt too fafting next morning; not furnifht
with beds apt to be defil'd, but more neceffary imple-
ments, Stooles, Table, and a Chamber-pot. It is a
broacher of more newes then hogs-heads, and more
iefts then newes, which are fuckt vp heere by fome
fpungy braine, and from thence fqueaz'd into a Comedy.
Men come heere to make merry, but indeed make a
noife, and this Muficke aboue is anfwered with the
clinking below. The Drawers are the ciuilleft people
in it, men of good bringing vp, and howfoeuer wee
efteeme of them, none can boaft more iuftly of their
high calling. Tis the beft Theater of natures, where
they are truely acted, not plaid, and the bufines as
in the reft of the world vp and downe, to wit, from
the bottome of the Seller to the great Chamber. A
melancholy Man would finde heere matter to worke
vpon, to fee Heads as brittle as Glaffes, and ofter
broken. Men come hither to quarrell, and come
hither to be made friends, and if *Plutarch* will lend
me his S[i]mile, it is euen *Telephus* his fword that makes
wounds, and cures them. It 'is the common confump

tion of the Afternoone, and the murderer, or maker away of a rainy day. It is the Torrid Zone that fcorches the face, and Tobacco the gun-power that blowes it vp. Much harme would be done, if the charitable Vintener had not Water readie for thefe flames. A houfe of finne you may call it, but not a houfe of darkeneffe, for the Candles are neuer out, and it is like thofe Countries farre in the North, where it is as cleare at mid-night as at mid-day. After a long fitting, it becomes like a ftreet in a dafhing fhowre, where the fpouts are flufhing aboue, and the Conduits running below, while the Iordans like fwelling riuers ouerflow their bankes. To giue you the totall reckoning of it. It is the bufie mans recreation, the idle mans bufineffe, the melancholy mans Sanctuary, the ftrangers welcome, the Innes a Court mans entertainment, the Scholers kindneffe, and the Citizens curtefie. It is the ftudie of fparkling wits, and a cup of Canary their booke, where we leaue them.

13. *A too idly referu'd Man*

IS one that is a foole with difcretion: or a ftrange piece of Politician, that manages the ftate of himfelfe. His Actions are his Priuie Counfell, wherein no man muft partake befide. He fpeakes vnder rule and prefcription, and dare not fhew his teeth without *Machiauell.* He conuerfes with his neighbours as hee would in Spaine, and feares an inquifitiue man as much as the Inquifition. He fufpects all queftions for examinations, and thinks you would pick fome thing out of him, and auoids you: His breft is lik[e] a gentlewomans clofet, which locks vp euerie toye and trifle, or fome bragging Mounte-banke, that makes euerie ftinking thing a fecret. He deliuers you common matters with great coniuration of filence, and whifpers you in the eare Acts of Parliament. You may as foone wreft a tooth from him as a paper, and whatſoeuer he reads is letters. Hee dares not talke of great men for feare of bad Comments, and hee knowes not how his words may bee miſapplyed. Aske his opinion and he tels you his doubt: and hee neuer heares any thing more aſtoniſhtly then what hee knowes before. His words are like the Cards at Primuiſte, where 6. is 18. and 7. 21. for they neuer ſignifie what they found; but if he tell you he wil do a thing, it is as much as if hee ſwore hee would not. He is one indeed that takes all men to be craftier then they are, and puts himſelfe to a great deale of affliction to hinder their plots, and deſignes where they meane freely. Hee ha's beene long a riddle himſelfe, but at laſt finds *Oedipuſſes*; for his ouer-acted diſſimulation diſcouers him, and men doe with him as they would with Hebrew letter, ſpell him backwards, and read him.

14. *A Sharke.*

IS one whome all other meanes haue fayl'd, and hee now liues of himſelfe. He is ſome needy chaſhir'd fellow, whom the World has oft flung off, yet ſtill claſpes againe, and is like one a drowning, faſtens vpon any thing that's next at hand, amongſt other of his Shipwrackes hee has happyly loſt ſhame, and this want ſupplies him. No man puts his Braine to more vſe then hee, for his life is a dayly inuention, and each meale a new ſtratagem. Hee has an excellent memorie for his acquaintance, though there paſt but how doe you betwixt them ſeuen yeeres agoe, it ſhall ſuffice for an Imbrace, and that for money. He offers you a Pottle of Sacke out of his ioy to ſee you, and in requitall of this courteſie, you can doe no leſſe then pay for it. He is fumbling with his purſe-ſtringes, as a Schoole-boy with his points, when hee is going to bee Whipt, till the Maſter wearie with long Stay, forgiues him. When the reckoning is payd, he ſayes it muſt not bee ſo, it [yet] is ſtrait pacified, and cryes what remedie.

His borrowings are like Subſidies, each man a ſhilling
or two, as hee can well diſpend, which they lend him,
not with the hope to be repayed, but that he wil
come no more. He holds a ſtrange tyranny ouer
men, for he is their debtor, and they feare him as a
creditor. He is proud of any imployment, though it
bee but to carry commendations, which he will be
ſure to deliuer at eleuen of the clocke. They in cur-
teſie bid him ſtay, and he in manners cannot deny
them. If he find but a good looke to aſſure his welcom, he becomes their halfe boorder, and haunts the
threſhhold ſo long, till he forces good naturs to the
neceſſity of a quarrell. Publique inuitations hee will
not wrong with his abſence, and is the beſt witneſſe
of the Sheriffes Hoſpitality. Men ſhun him at length
as they would doe an infection, and he is neuer croſt
in his way, if there be but a lane to eſcape him. He
ha's done with the Age as his clothes to him, hung on
as long as hee could, and at laſt drops off.

15. *A Carryer*

IS his own Hackneyman for hee lets himſelfe out to trauell as well as his horſes.
Hee is the ordinarie Embaſſadour betweene Friend and Friend, and brings rich
Preſents to the one, but neuer returnes any
backe againe. He is no vnletter'd man, though in
ſhew ſimple, for queſtionleſſe, hee has much in his
Budget, which hee can vtter too in fit time and place;
Hee is the Vault in Gloſter Church, that conueyes
Whiſpers at a diſtance; for hee takes the ſound out
of your mouth at Yorke, and makes it bee heard as
farre as London. Hee is the young Students ioy and
expectation, and the moſt accepted gueſt, to whom
they lend a willing hand to diſcharge him of his burthen. His firſt greeting is, Your Friends are well;
then in a piece of Gold deliuers their Bleſſing. You
would thinke him a Churliſh blunt fellow, but they

find in him many tokens of humanitie. He is a great afflicter of the High-way, and beates them out of mesure, which iniury is somtimes reuengd by the Purse taker; and then the Voyage miscaries. No man domineers more in his Inne, nor cals his Host vnreuerently with more presumption, and this arrogance proceeds out of the strength of his Horses. He forgets not his load where he takes his ease, for he is drunke commonly before he goes to bed. He is like the Prodigall Child, still packing away, and still returning againe. But let him passe.

16. *An old Colledge Butler.*

IS none of the worst Students in the house, for he keepes the set houres at his booke more duly then any. His authority is great ouer mens good names, which hee charges many times with shrewd aspersions, which they hardly wipe off without payment. His Boxe and Counters proue him to be a man of reckoning; yet hee is stricter in his accounts then a Vsurer, and deliuers not a farthing without writing. He doubles the paine of *Gallobelgicus*, for his bookes goe out once a quarter, and they are much in the same nature, briefe notes and summes of affaires, and are out of request as soone. His commings in are like a Taylors from the shreds of bread, the chippings, and remnants of the broken crust: excepting his vailes from the barrell, which poore folkes buy for their hogs, but drinke themselues. He diuides a halfepeny loafe with more subtilty then *Kekerman*, and sub-diuides the *a primo ortum* so nicely, that a stomacke of great capacity can hardly apprehend it. Hee is a very sober man considering his manifold temptations of drinke and strangers, and if hee be ouer-seene, tis within his owne liberties, and no man ought to take exceptions. He is neuer so well pleas'd with his place, as when a Gentleman is beholding to him for shewing him the

Buttery, whom hee greets with a cup of ſingle beere
and flyſt manchet, and tels him tis the faſhion of the
Colledge. Hee domineers ouer Freſhmen when they
firſt come to the Hatch, and puzzles them with ſtrange
language of Cues, and Cees, and ſome broken Latine
which he ha's learnt at his Bin. His faculties extraordinary, is the warming of a paire of Cards, and telling out a doozen of Counters for Poſt and Paire, and
no man is more methodicall in theſe buſineſſes. Thus
hee ſpends his age, till the tappe of it is runne out,
and then a freſh one is ſet abroach.

17. *An Vp-ſtart Countrey Knight.*

Is honour was ſomewhat prepoſterous, for
hee bare the Kings ſword before he had
armes to wield it; yet being once laid
ore the ſhoulder with a Knighthood, he
finds the Herauld his friend. His father
was a man of good ſtocke, though but a Tanner,
or Vſuter; hee purchaſt the Land, and his ſon the
Title. He ha's doft off the name of a Clowne, but the
looke not ſo eaſie, and his face beares ſtill a reliſh of
Churne-milke. Hee is garded with more Gold lace
then all the Gentlemen o' th Countrie, yet his body
makes his clothes ſtil out of faſhion. His houſekeep-
ing is ſeene much in the diſtinct families of Dogges,
and Seruing-men attendant on their kennels, and the
deepeneſſe of their throats is the depth of his diſcourſe.
A Hauke hee eſteemes the true burthen of Nobilitie,
and is exceeding ambitious to ſeeme delighted in the
ſport, and haue his fiſt Glou'd with his Ieſſes. A Iuſtice
of peace hee is to domineere in his Pariſh, and doe
his neighbour wrong with more right. And very ſcandalous hee is in his authoritie, for no ſinne almoſt
which hee will not commit. Hee will bee drunke
with his hunters for companie, and ſtaine his Gentilitie
with droppings of Ale. He is fearefull of being Sheriffe
of the Shire by inſtinct, and dreads the Size-weeke as

much as the Prifoner. In fumme, he is but a clod of
his owne earth; or his Land is the Dunghill, and he
the Cocke that crowes ouer it. And commonly his
race is quickely runne, and his Childrens Children,
though they fcape hanging, returne to the place from
whence they came.

18. *A Gallant.*

IS one that was born and fhapt for his
Cloathes: and if *Adam* had not falne, had
liu'd to no purpofe. Hee gratulates therefore the firft finne, and fig leaues that
were an occafion of brauerie. His firft care
is his dreffe, the next his bodie, and in the vniting
of thefe two lies his foule and its faculties. Hee
obferues London trulier then the Termers, and his
bufineffe is the ftreet: the Stage the Court, and thofe
places where a proper man is beft fhowne. If hee be
qualified in gaming extraordinary, he is fo much the
more gentle and compleate, and hee learnes the beaft
[beft] oathes for the purpofe. Thefe are a great part of
his difcourfe, and he is as curious in their newneffe as
the fafhion. His other talke is Ladies and fuch pretty
things, or fome ieft at a Play. His Pick-tooth beares
a great part in his difcourfe, fo does his body; the
vpper parts whereof are as ftarcht as his linnen, and
perchance vfe the fame Laundreffe. Hee has learnt
to ruffle his face from his Boote, and takes great delight in his walke to heare his Spurs gingle. Though
his life paffe fomewhat flidingly, yet he feemes very
carefull of the time, for hee is ftill drawing his Watch
out of his Poket, and fpends part of his houres in
numbring them. He is one neuer ferious but with
his Taylor, when hee is in confpiracie for the next
deuice. He is furnifht [with] his Iefts, as fome wanderer
with Sermons, fome three for all Congregations, one
efpecially againft the Scholler, a man to him much
ridiculous, whome hee knowes by no other definition,
but a filly fellow in blacke. He is a kind of walking

Mercers Shop, and ſhewes you one Stuffe to day, and
another to morrow, an ornament to the roomes he
comes in, as the faire bed and Hangings be ; and is
meerely ratable accordingly, fiftie or an hundred Pound
as his ſuit is. His maine ambition is to get a Knight
hood, and then an olde Ladie, which if he be happy
in, he fils the Stage and a Coach ſo much longer.
Otherwiſe, himſelfe and his Cloathes grow ſtale together, and he is buried commonly ere hee dies in
the Gaole, or the Country.

19. *A Conſtable*

IS a Vice-roy in the ſtreet, and no man
ſtands more vpon't that he is the Kings
Officer. His Iuriſdiction extends to the
next ſtocks, where hee ha's Commiſſion
for the heeles only, and ſets the reſt of
the body at libertie. Hee is a ſcar-crow to that Ale-
houſe, where he drinkes not his mornings draught, and
apprehends a Drunkard for not ſtanding in the Kings
name. Beggers feare him more than the Iuſtice, and
as much as the Whip ſtocke, whom hee deliuers ouer
to his ſubordinate Magiſtrates, the Bride-wel-man, and
the Beadle. Hee is a great ſtickler in the tumults of
double Iugges, and venters his head by his Place,
which is broke many times to keep whole the peace.
He is neuer ſo much in his Maieſty as in his Night-
watch, where hee ſits in his Chayre of State, a Shop-
ſtall, and inuiron'd with a guard of Halberts, examines
all paſſengers. Hee is a very carefull man in his Office,
but if hee ſtay vp after Midnight, you ſhall take him
napping.

20. *A downe-right Scholler*

IS one that has much learning in the Ore,
vnwrought and vntryde, which time and
experience faſhions and refines. He is
good mettall in the inſide, though rough
and vnſcour'd without, and therefore hated

of the Courtier, that is quite contrarie. The time
has got a veine of making him ridiculous, and men
laugh at him by tradition, and no vnluckie abfur-
dity, but is put vpon his profeffion, and done like a
Scholler. But his fault is onely this, that his minde is
fomewhat much taken vp with his mind, and his
thoughts not loaden with any carriage befides. Hee
has not put on the quaint Garbe of the Age, which is
now become a mans Totall. He has not humbled his
Meditations to the induftrie of Complement, nor
afflicted his braine in an elaborate legge. His body
is not fet vpon nice Pinnes, to bee turning and flexible
for euery motion, but his fcrape is homely, and his
nod worfe. He cannot kiffe his hand and cry Madame,
nor talke. idly enough to beare her company. His
fmacking of a Gentle-woman is fomewhat too fauory,
and he miftakes her nofe for her lippe. A very Wood-
cocke would puzzle him in caruing, and hee wants the
logicke of a Capon. He has not the glib faculty of
fliding ouer a tale, but his words come squeamifhly
out of his mouth, and the laughter commonly before
the ieft. He names this word Colledge too often, and
his difcourfe beats too much on the Vniuerfity. The
perplexity of mannerlineffe will not let him feed, and
he is fharpe fet at an argument when hee fhould cut
his meate. He is difcarded for a gamefter at all
games but one and thirty, and at tables he reaches
not beyond doublets. His fingers are not long and
drawn out to handle a Fiddle, but his fift is cluncht
with the habite of difputing. Hee afcends a horfe
fomwhat finifterly, though not on the left fide, and
they both goe iogging in griefe together. He is exceedingly cenfur'd by the Innes a Court men, for that
hainous Vice being out of fafhion. Hee cannot
fpeake to a Dogge in his owne Dialect, and vnderftands
Greeke better then the language of a Falconer. Hee
has beene vfed to a darke roome, and darke Clothes,
and his eyes dazzle at a Sattin Doublet. The Her-
mitage of his Study, has made him fom what vncouth

in the world, and men make him worfe by ftaring on
him. Thus is hee filly and ridiculous, and it continues
with him for fome quarter of a yeare, out of the Vniuerſitie. But practife him a little in men, and bruſh
him ore with good companie, and hee ſhall out ballance thofe glifterers as much as a folid fubftance do's
a feather, or Gold Gold-lace.

21. *A Player.*

HE knowes the right vfe of the World,
wherein hee comes to play a part and
so away, His life is not idle for it is all
Action, and no man need be more wary
in his doings, for the eyes of all men are
vpon him. His profeffion ha's in it a kind of contra-
diction, for none is more diſlik'd, and yet none more
applauded and hee ha's this misfortune of fome Scholler, too much witte makes him a foole. He is like
our painting Gentle-women, feldome in his owne
face, feldomer in his cloathes, and hee pleafes, the
better hee counterfeits, except onely when hee is difguis'd with ftraw for gold lace. Hee do's nct only
perfonate on the Stage, but fometime in the Street, for
hee is maskd ftill in the habite of a Gentleman. His
Parts find him oathes and good words, which he
keepes for his vfe and Difcourfe, and makes fhew with
them of a fafhionable Companion. He is tragicall on
the Stage, but rampant in the Tyring-houfe, and fweares
oathes there which he neuer con'd. The waiting
women Spectators are ouer-eares in loue with him, and
Ladies fend for him to act in their Chambers. Your
Innes of Court men were vndone but for him, hee is
their chiefe gueft and imployment, and the fole bufi-
nefle that makes them After-noones men; The Poet
only is his Tyrant, and hee is bound to make his
friends friend drunk at his charges. Shroue-tuefday
hee feares as much as the Baudes, and Lent is more
damage to him then the Butcher. Hee was neuer fo

much difcredited as in one Act, and that was of Parliament, which giues Hoftlers Priuiledge before him, for which hee abhors it more then a corrupt Iudge. But to giue him his due, one wel-furnifht Actor has enough in him for fiue common Gentlemen, and if he haue a good body for fixe, and for refolution, hee fhall Challenge any *Cato*, for it has beene his practife to die brauely.

22. *A Detractor*

IS one of a more cunning and actiue enuy, wherewith he gnaws not foolifhly himfelfe, but throwes it abroad and would haue it blifter others. He is commonly fome weake parted fellow, and worfe minded, yet is ftrangely ambitious to match others, not by mounting their worth, but bringing them downe with his Tongue to his owne pooreneffe. Hee is indeed like the red Dragon that purfued the woman, for when hee cannot ouerreach another, hee opens his mouth and throwes a flood after to drowne him. You cannot anger him worfe then to doe well, and hee hates you more bitterly for this, then if you had cheated him of his patrimony with your owne difcredit. He is always flighting the generall opinion, and wondring why fuch and fuch men fhould bee applauded. Commend a good Diuine, hee cryes Poftilling; a Philologer, Pedantrie; a Poet, Ryming; a Schoole-man, dull wrangling; a fharpe conceit, Boy-ifhneffe; an honeft Man, plaufibilitie. Hee comes to publique things not to learne, but to catch, and if there bee but one folœcifme, that's all he carries away. Hee lookes on all things with a prepared fowreneffe, and is ftill furnifht with a Pifh before hand, or fome mufty Prouerbe that dif-relifhes all things whatfoeuer. If feare of the company make him fecond a commendation, it is like a Law-writ, alwaies with a claufe and exception, or to fmooth his way to fome greater fcandall. Hee will grant you something, and bate more; and this bating ſhal in conclusion take away all hee granted. His ſpeech concludes ſtill with an Oh but, and I could wiſh one thing amended; and this one thing ſhal be enough to deface all his former commendations. Hee will bee very inward with a man to fiſh ſome bad out of him, and make his ſlanders hereafter more authenticke, when it is ſaid a friend reported it. Hee will inueigle you to naughtineſſe to get your good name into his clutches, and make you drunk to ſhew you reeling. Hee paſſes the more plauſibly becauſe all men haue a ſmatch of his humour, and it is thought freenes which is malice. If hee can ſay nothing of a man, hee will ſeeme to ſpeake riddles, as if he could tell ſtrange ſtories if hee would: and when hee has rackt his inuention to the vttermoſt, hee ends: But I wiſh him well, and therefore muſt hold my peace. Hee is alwayes liſtning and enquiring after men, and ſuffers not a cloake to paſſe by him vnexamin'd. In briefe, hee is one that has loſt all good himſelfe, and is loth to finde it in another.

23. *A meere young Gentleman of the Vniuerſitie*

IS one that comes there to weare a gowne, and to ſay hereafter, hee has beene at the Vniuerſitie. His Father ſent him thither, becauſe hee heard there were the beſt Fencing and Dancing Schooles, from theſe he has his Education, from his Tutor the ouerſight. The firſt Element of his knowledge is to be ſhewne the Colledges, and initiated in a Tauerne by the way, which hereafter hee will learne of himſelfe. The two markes of his Senioritie, is the bare Veluet of his gowne, and his proficiencie at Tennis, where when hee can once play a Set, he is a Freſh-man no more. His Studie has commonly handſome Shelues, his Bookes neate Silke ſtrings, which hee ſhewes to his

Fathers man, and is loth to vntye or take downe for feare of misplacing. Vpon foule dayes for recreation hee retyres thither, and looks ouer the prety booke his Tutor Reades to him, which is commonly some short Historie, or a piece of *Euphormio;* for which his Tutor giues him Money to spend next day. His maine loytering is at the Library, where hee studies Armes and bookes of Honour, and turnes a Gentleman-Critick in Pedigrees. Of all things hee endures not to be mistaken for a Scholler, and hates a black suit though it bee of Sattin. His companion is ordinarily some stale fellow, that ha's beene notorious for an Ingle to gold hatbands, whom hee admires at first, afterward scornes. If hee haue spirit or wit, hee may light of better company, and may learne some flashes of wit, which may doe him Knights seruice in the Country hereafter. But hee is now gone to the Inns of Court, where hee studies to forget what hee learn'd before, his acquaintance and the fashion.

24. *A Pot-Poet*

IS the dreggs of wit; yet mingled with good drinke may haue some relish. His Inspirations are more reall then others; for they doe but faine a God, but hee has his by him. His Verses run like the Tap, and his inuention as the Barrell, ebs and flowes at the mercy of the spiggot. In thin drinke hee aspires not aboue a Ballad, but a cup of Sacke inflames him, and sets his Muse and Nose a fire together. The Presse is his Mint, and stamps him now and then a sixe pence or two in reward of the baser coyne his Pamphlet. His workes would scarce sell for three halfe pence, though they are giuen oft for three Shillings, but for the pretty Title that allures the Country Gentleman: and for which the Printer maintaines him in Ale a fortnight. His Verses are like his clothes, miserable Cento's and patches, yet their pace is not altogether so hobling as an Almanacks. The death of a great man or the burning of a house furnish him with an Argument, and the nine Muses are out strait in mourning gowne, and *Melpomine cryes* Fire, Fire, His other Poems are but Briefs in Rime, and like the poore Greekes collections to redeeme from captiuity. He is a man now much imploy'd in commendations of our Nauy, and a bitter inueigher against the Spaniard. His frequent'st Workes goe out in single sheets, and are chanted from market to market, to a vile tune, and a worse throat: whilst the poore Country wench melts like her butter to heare them. And these are the Stories of some men of Tiburne, or a strange Monster out of Germany: or sitting in a Baudy-house, hee writes Gods Iudgements. Hee ends at last in some obscure painted Cloth, to which himselfe made the Verses, and his life like a Canne too full spils vpon the bench. He leaues twenty shillings on the score, which my Hostesse looses.

25. *A Cooke.*

He Kitchin is his Hell, and hee the Diuell in it, where his meate and he frye together. His Reuennues are showr'd downe from the fat of the Land, and he enterlards his owne grease among to helpe the drippings. Colericke hee is, not by nature so much as his Art, and it is a shrewd temptation that the chopping knife is so neare. His weapons ofter offensiue, are a messe of hot broth and scalding water, and woe bee to him that comes in his way. In the Kitchin he will domineere, and rule the roste, in spight of his Master, and Curses is the very Dialect of his Calling. His labour is meere blustring and furie, and his Speech like that of Sailors in a storme, a thousand businesses at once, yet in all this tumult hee do's not loue combustion, but will bee the first man that shall goe and quench it. Hee is neuer good Christian till a hizzing

Pot of Ale has flak't him, like Water caſt on a fire-
brand, and for that time hee is tame and difpoſſeſt.
His cunning is not ſmall in Architecture, for hee builds
ſtrange Fabricks in Paſte, Towres and Caſtles, which
are offered to the aſſault of valiant teeth, and like
Darius his Pallace, in one Banquet demoliſht. Hee
is a pittileſſe murderer of Innocents, and hee mangles
poore foules with vnheard of tortures, and it is thought
the Martyrs perſecutions were deuiſed from hence,
ſure we are Saint *Lawrence* his Gridiron came out of
his Kitchin. His beſt facultie is at the Dreſſer, where
hee ſeemes to haue great skill in the Tractikes, ranging
his Diſhes in order, Militarie: and placing with great
difcretion in the fore-front meates more ſtrong and
hardy and the more cold and cowardly in the reare,
as quaking Tarts, and quiuering Cuſtards, and ſuch
milke ſop Diſhes which ſcape many times the fury
of the encounter. But now the ſecond Courſe is
gone vp, and hee downe into the Sellar, where hee
drinkes and ſleepes till foure a clocke in the afternoone, and then returnes againe to his Regiment.

26. *A forward bold Man*

IS a luſty fellow in a crowd, that's beholding more to his elbow then his legges, for
he do's not go, but thruſts well. Hee is
a good ſhuffler in the world, wherein he
is ſo oft putting forth, that at length he puts
on. He can doe ſomething, but dare doe much more,
and is like a deſperate ſoldier, who will aſſault any
thing where hee is ſure not to enter. He is not ſo
well opinion'd of himſelfe, as induſtrious to make other;
and thinke [thinks] no vice ſo preiudiciall as bluſhing.
Hee is ſtill citing for himſelfe, that a candle ſhould
not be hid vnder a buſhell, and for his part, he will be
ſure not to hide his, though his candle bee but a ſnuffe
or Ruſh-candle. Theſe few good parts hee has, hee
is no niggard in diſplaying, and is like ſome needy

flanting Gold-fmith, no thing in the inner roome, but
all on the cup-boord: If he be a fcholler, he ha's
commonly flept into the Pulpit before a degree; yet
into that too before he deferu'd it. Hee neuer de-
ferres St. *Maries* beyond his regencie, and his next
Sermon is at *Pauls* Croffe, and that printed. He loues
publike things alife: and for any folemne entertainment he will find a mouth, find a fpeech who will.
Hee is greedy of great acquaintance and many, and
thinkes it no fmall aduancement to rife to bee knowne.
His talke at the table is like *Beniamins* meffe, fiue
times to his part, and no argument fhuts him out for a
quarrellour. Of all difgraces he indures not to bee *Non-
pluft*, and had rather flye for Sanctuary to *Non fenfe*,
which few can defcry, then to nothing which all. His
boldneffe is beholding to other mens modeftie, which
refcues him many times from a Baffle, yet his face is
good Armour, and hee is dafht out of any thing fooner
then Countenance. Groffer conceites are puzzel'd in
him for a rare man, and wifer men, though they know
him, take him for their pleafure, or as they would doe
a Sculler for being next at hand. Thus preferment at
laft ftumbles on him bicaufe, hee is ftill in the way.
His Companions that flouted him before, now enuie
him, when they fee him come readie for Scarlet, whilft
themfelues lye Muftie in their old Clothes and Colledges.

27. *A Baker.*

NO man verifies the Prouerbe more, that it
is an Almef-deed to punifh him: for his
penalty is a Dole, and do's the Beggers
as much good as their Dinner. He abhors therefore workes of Charitie, and
thinkes his Bread caft away when it is giuen to the
poore. He loues not Iuftice neither, for the weigh-
fcales fake, and hates the Clarke of the Market as his
Executioner: yet hee findes mercy in his offences,

and his Basket onely is fent to Prifon. Marry a Pillory is his deadly enemy, and he neuer heares well after.

28. *A plaine Country Fellow*

IS one that manures his ground well, but lets himfelfe lie fallow and vntil'd. Hee has reafon enough to doe his bufineffe, and not enough to bee idle or melancholy. Hee feemes to haue the iudgement of *Nabuchadnezar:* for his conuerfation is among beafts, and his tallons none of the fhorteft, only he eates not graffe, becaufe hee loues not fallets. His hand guides the Plough, and the Plough his thoughts, and his ditch and land-marke is the very mound of his meditations. He expoftulates with his Oxen very vnderftandingly, and fpeaks Gee and Ree better then Englifh. His mind is not much diftracted with obiects: but if a goode fat Cowe come in his way, he ftands dumbe and aftonifht, and though his hafte bee neuer fo great, will fixe here halfe an houres contemplation. His habitation is fome poore Thatcht roofe, diftinguifht from his Barn, by the loope-holes that let out fmoak, which the raine had long fince wafht thorow, but for the double feeling of Bacon on the infide, which has hung there from his Grandfires time, and is yet to make rafhers for pofterity. His Dinner is his other worke, for he fweats at it as much as at his labour; he is a terrible faftner on a piece of Beefe, and you may hope to ftaue the Guard off fooner. His Religion is a part of his Copy-hold, which hee takes from his Land-lord, and referres it wholly to his difcretion. Yet if hee giue him leaue, he is a good Chriftian to his power (that is) comes to Church in his beft clothes, and fits there with his Neighbours, where he is capable onely of two Prayers, for raines and faire weather. Hee apprehends Gods bleffings onely in a Good Yeere, or a Fat pafture, and neuer

praifes him but on good ground. Sunday he efteemes
a day to make merry in, and thinkes a Bag-pipe as
effentiall to it, as Euening-Prayer, where hee walkes
very folemnly after feruice with his hands coupled
behind him, and cenfures the dauncing of his parifh.
His complement with his Neighbour, is a good thumpe
on the backe; and his falutation, commonly fome
blunt Curfe. Hee thinks nothing to bee vices but
Pride and ill hufbandrie, for which hee wil grauely
diffwade youth and has fome thriftie Hobnayle Pro-
uerbes to Clout his difcourfe. He is a niggard all the
Weeke except onely Market-day, where if his Corne
fell well, hee thinkes hee may be drunke with a good
Confcience. His feete neuer ftincke fo vnbecom-
mingly, as when hee trots after a Lawyer in Weft-
minfter-hall, and euen cleaues the ground with hard
fcraping, in befeeching his Worfhip to take his money.
Hee is fenfible of no calamitie but the burning of a
Stacke of Corne, or the ouer-flowing of a Medow,
and thinkes *Noahs* Flood the greateft Plague that euer
was, not becaufe it Drowned the World, but fpoyl'd
the graffe. For Death hee is neuer troubled, and if
hee get in but his Harueft before, let it come when it
wil he cares not.

29. *A Young-man.*

Ee is now out of Natures protection, though
not yet able to guide himfelfe: But left
loofe to the World, and Fortune, from
which the weakneffe of his Childhood
preferu'd him: and now his ftrength ex-
pofes him. Hee is indeed iuft of age to be miferable, yet in his owne conceit firft begins to be happy;
and hee is happier in this imagination, and his mifery
not felt is leffe. He fees yet but the outfide of the
World and Men, and conceiues them according to their
appearing glifter, and out of this ignorance beleeues
them. He purfues all vanities for happineffe, and
enioyes them beft in this fancy. His reafon ferues

not to curbe, but vnderſtand his appetite, and proſecute the motions thereof with a more eager earneſtnes. Himſelfe is his owne temptation, and needs not Satan; and the World will come hereafter. Hee leaues repentance for gray hayres, and performes it in being couetous. Hee is mingled with the vices of the age as the faſhion and cuſtome, with which he longs to bee acquainted; and Sinnes to better his vnderſtanding. He conceiues his Youth as the ſeaſon of his Luſt, and the Houre wherein hee ought to bee bad: and becauſe he would not loſe his time, ſpends it. He diſtaſts Religion as a ſad thing, and is ſixe yeeres elder for a thought of Heauen. Hee ſcornes and feares, and yet hopes for old age, but dare not imagine it with wrincles. Hee loues and hates with the ſame inflamation: and when the heate is ouer, is coole alike to friends and enemies. His friendſhip is ſeldome ſo ſtedfaſt, but that luſt, drinke, or anger may ouerturne it. He offers you his blood to day in kindneſſe, and is readie to take yours to morrow. He do's ſeldome any thing which hee wiſhes not to doe againe, and is onely wiſe after a miſfortune. Hee ſuffers much for his knowledge, and a great deale of folly it is makes him a wiſe man. Hee is free from many Vices, by being not grown to the performance, and is onely more vertuous out of weakneſſe. Everie action is his danger, and euery man his ambuſh. Hee is a Shippe without Pilot or Tackling, and only good fortune may ſteere him. If hee ſcape this age, hee ha's ſcap't a Tempeſt, and may liue to be a Man.

30. *The common ſinging-men in Cathedrall Churches*

ARe a bad Society, and yet a Company of good Fellowes, that roare deep in the Quire deeper in the Tauerne. They are the eighth part of ſpeech, which goe to the Syntaxis of Seruice, and are diſtinguiſh't by their noyfes much like Bells, for they make not a Confort but a Peale. Their paftime or recreation is prayers, their exercife drinking, yet herein fo religioufly addicted that they ferue God ofteſt when they are drunke. Their humanity is a legge to the Refidencer, their learning a Chapter, for they learne it commonly before they read it, yet the old Hebrew names are little beholding to them, for they mif-call them worfe then one another. Though they neuer expound the Scripture, they handle it much, and pollute the Gofpell with two things, their Conuerfation, and their thumbes. Vpon Worky-dayes they behaue themfelues at Prayers as at their Pots, for they fwallow them downe in an inftant. Their Gownes are lac'd commonly with ftreamings of Ale, the fuperfluites of cups or throat aboue meafure. Their skill in melody makes them the better companions abroad, and their Anthemes abler to fing Catches. Long-liu'd for the moft part they are not, efpecially the bafe, they ouer flow their banke fo oft to drowne the Organs. Briefly, if they efcape arrefting, they dye conftantly in Gods Seruice ; and to eake [take] their death with more patience, they haue Wine and Cakes at their Funerall : and now they keepe the Church a great deale better, and helpe to fill it with their bones as before with their noife.

31. *A Pretender to Learning*

IS one that would make others more fooles then himfelfe; for though he know nothing, he would not haue the world know fo much. He conceits nothing in Learning but the opinion, which he feekes to purchafe without it, though hee might with leffe labour cure his ignorance, then hide it. He is indeed a kind of Scholler-Mountebank, and his Art, our delufion. He is trickt out in all the accoutrements of Learning, and at the firft encounter none paffes better. Hee is oftner in his ſtudy, then at his Booke, and you cannot pleaſure him better, then to deprehend him. Yet he heares you not till the third knocke, and then comes out very angry, as interrupted. You find him in his Slippers, and a Pen in his eare, in which formality he was aſleep. His Table is ſpred wide with ſome Claſſicke Folio, which is as conſtant to it as the carpet, and hath laid open in the ſame Page this half yeere. His Candle is alwayes a longer ſitter vp then himſelfe, and the boaſt of his Window at Midnight. He walkes much alone in the Poſture of Meditation, and ha's a Booke ſtill before his face in the fields. His pocket is ſeldome without a Greeke Teſtament, or Hebrew Bible, which hee opens only in the Church, and that when ſome ſtander by lookes ouer. He has his ſentences for Company, ſome ſcatterings of *Seneca* and *Tacitus*, which are good vpon all occaſions. If he read any thing in the morning, it comes vp all at dinner: and as long as that laſts, the diſcourſe is his. Hee is a great *Plagiarie* of Tauerne-wit: and comes to Sermons onely that hee may talke of *Auſtin*. His Parcels are the meere ſcrapings from Company, yet he complains at parting what time he has loſt. He is wondrouſly capricious to ſeeme a iudgement, and liſtens with a ſowre attention, to what hee vnderſtands not. Hee talkes much of *Scaliger* and *Cauſabone*, and the Ieſuites, and prefers ſome vnheard-of Dutch name before them all. He has verſes to bring in vpon theſe and theſe hints, and it ſhall goe hard but he will wind in his opportunity. Hee is criticall in a language hee cannot conſter, and ſpeaks ſeldome vnder *Arminius* in Diuinity. His buſineſſe and retirement and caller away is his Study, and he proteſts no delight to it comparable. Hee is a great Nomen-clator of Authors, which hee has read in generall in the Catalogue, and in particular in the Title, and goes ſeldome ſo farre as the Dedication. Hee neuer talkes of any thing but learning, and learnes all from talking. Three in-counters with the same men pumpe him, and then hee onely puts in, or grauely sayes nothing. He ha's taken paines to be an Asse, though not to be a Scholler, and is at length discouered and laught at.

32. *A Shop-keeper.*

Is Shop is his well stuft Booke, and himselfe the Title-page of it, or Index. Hee vtters much to all men, though he sels but to a few, and intreats for his owne necessities by asking others what they lacke. No man speakes more and no more, for his words are like his Wares, twentie of one sort, and he goes ouer them alike to all commers. Hee is an arrogant commender of his owne things; for whatsoeuer hee shewes you, is the best in the Towne, though the worst in his Shop. His Conscience was a thing, that would haue layde vpon his hands, and he was forc't to put it off: and makes great vse of honestie to professe vpon. Hee tels you lyes by rote, and not minding, as the Phrase to sell in, and the Language hee spent most of his yeeres to learne. He neuer speakes so truely, as when hee sayes hee would vse you as his Brother, for hee would abuse his brother; and in his Shop, thinkes it lawfull. His Religion is much in the nature of his Customers, and indeed the Pander to it: and by a misinterpreted sense of Scripture makes a gaine of his Godlinesse. Hee is your slaue while you pay him ready Money, but if hee once befriend you, your Tyrant, and you had better deserue his hate then his trust.

33. *A handsome Hostesse*

S the fairer commendation of an Inne, aboue the faire Signe or faire Lodgings. She is the Loadstone that attracts men of Iron, Gallants and Roarers, where they cleaue sometimes long, and are not easily got off.

Her Lips are your wel-come, and your entertainement
her companie, which is put into the reckoning too,
and is the deareſt parcell in it: No Citizens wife is
demurer then ſhee at the firſt greeting, nor drawes in
her mouth with a chaſter ſimper, but you may be more
familiar without diſtaſte, and ſhee do's not ſtartle at
Baudry. She is the confuſion of a Pottle of Sacke
more then would haue beene ſpent elſ-where, and her
litle Iugs are accepted, to haue her Kiſſe excuſe them.
Shee may be an honeſt woman, but is not beleeu'd ſo
in her Pariſh, and no man is a greater Infidel in it
then her Husband.

34. *A Blunt Man*

IS one whoſe wit is better pointed then his
behauiour, and that courſe, and Impolliſht
not out of ignorance ſo much as humour.
He is a great enemy to the fine Gentleman, and theſe things of Complement,
and hates ceremonie in conuerſation, as the Puritan
in Religion. Hee diſtinguiſhes not betwixt faire
and double-dealing, and ſuſpects all ſmoothneſſe for
the dreſſe of knauerie. Hee ſtarts at the encounter
of a Salutation, as an aſſault, and beſeeches you in
choller to forbeare your courteſie. Hee loues not any
thing in Diſcourſe that comes before the purpoſe, and
is alwaies ſuſpicious of a Preface. Himſelfe falls
rudely ſtill on his matter without any circumſtance,
except hee vſe an old Prouerbe for an Introduction.
Hee ſweares olde out of date innocent othes, as by
the Maſſe, by our Ladie, and ſuch like, and though
there bee Lords preſent, he cryes, My Maſters. Hee
is exceedingly in loue with his Humour, which makes
him alwayes profeſſe and proclaime it, and you muſt
take what he ſayes patiently, becauſe he is a plaine
man. His nature is his excuſe ſtill, and other mens
Tyrant: for hee muſt ſpeake his mind, and that is his
worſt, and craues your pardon moſt iniuriouſly for not

pardoning you. His Iefts beft become him, becaufe they come from him rudely and vnaffected: and hee has the lucke commonly to haue them famous. Hee is one that will doe more then he will fpeake, and yet fpeake more then hee will heare: for though hee loue to touch others, hee is teachy himfelfe, and feldome to his own abufes replyes but with his Fifts. Hee is as fqueazy of his commendations as his courtefie, and his good word is like an Elogie in a Satyre. Hee is generally better fauour'd then hee fauours, as being commonly well expounded in his bitterneffe, and no man fpeakes treafon more fecurely. Hee chides great men with moft boldneffe, and is counted for it an honeft fellow. Hee is grumbling much in the behalfe of the Commonwealth, and is in Prifon oft for it with credit. Hee is generally honeft, but more generally thought fo, and his downe rightneffe credits him, as a man not wel bended and crookned to the times. In conclufion, hee is not eafily bad, in whom this qualitie is Nature, but the counterfeit is moft dangerous fince hee is difguis'd in a humour, that profeffes not to difguife.

35. *A Criticke*

IS one that has fpeld ouer a great many of Bookes, and his obferuation is the Orthographie. Hee is the Surgeon of old Authors, and heales the wounds of duft and ignorance. He conuerfes much in fragments and *Defunt multa's*, and if he piece it vp with two Lines, he is more proud of that Booke then the Authour. Hee runnes ouer all Sciences to perufe their Syntaxis, and thinkes all Learning compris'd in writing Latine. Hee taftes Styles, as fome difcreeter Palats doe Wine; and tels you which is Genuine, which Sophifticate and baftard. His owne Phrafe is a Mifcellany of old words, deceas'd long before the *Cæfars*, and entoomb'd by *Varro*, and the modern'ft man hee followes, is *Plautus*. Hee writes *Omneis* at length, and *quicquid*, and his Gerund is moft inconformable. Hee is a trouble troublefome vexer of the dead, which after fo long fparing muft rife vp to the Iudgement of his caftigations. He is one that makes all Bookes fell dearer, whilft he fwels them into Folio's with his Comments.

36. *A Sergeant or Catch-pole*

Is one of Gods Iudgements; and which our Roarers doe onely conceiue terrible. Hee is the propereft fhape wherein they fancie Satan; for hee is at moft but an Arrefter, and Hell a Dungeon. Hee is the Creditors Hawke, wherewith they feaze vpon flying Birds, and fetch them againe in his Tallons. He is the Period of young Gentlemen, or their full ftop, for when hee meets with them they can go no farther. His Ambufh is a Shop Stall, or clofe Lane, and his Affault is cowardly at your backe. He refpites you in no place but a Tauerne, where he fels his Minutes dearer then a Clocke-maker. The common way to runne from him, is through him, which is often attempted and atchieued, and no man is ofter beaten out of Charitie. He is one makes the ftreete more dangerous then the High-wayes, and men goe better prouided in their walkes then their Iourney. Hee is the firft handfell of the young Rapiers of the Templers, and they are as proud of his repulfe, as an Hungarian of killing a Turke. He is a moueable Prifon, and his hands two Manacles hard to be fil'd off. Hee is an occafioner of difloyall thoughts in the Commonwealth, for he makes men hate the Kings Name worfe then the Deuils.

37. *A weake Man*

IS one whom Nature huddled vp in hafte, and left his beft part vnfinifh't. The reft of him is growne to bee a man, onely his braine ftayes behind. Hee is a man that ha's not improou'd his firft rudiments, nor attain'd any proficiencie by his ftay in the world : but wee may fpeake of him yet, as when hee was in the budde, a goode harmeleffe nature, a well meaning mind, if hee could order his intentions. It is his mifery that hee now moft wants a Tutor, and is too old to haue one. Hee is two fteps aboue a foole, and a great many mo below a wife-man: yet the foole is oft giuen him, and by thofe whom he efteems moft. Some tokens of him are : Hee loues men better vpon relation then experience : for he is exceedingly enamour'd of Strangers, and none quicklier a weary of his friends. Hee charges you at firft meeting with all his fecrets, and on better acquaintance growes more referu'd. Indeed hee is one that miftakes much his abufers for friends, and his friends for enemies, and hee apprehends your hate in nothing fo much, as in good counfell. One that is flexible with any thing but reafon, and then only peruerfe; and you may better intice then perfwade him. A feruant to euery tale and flatterer, and whom the laft man ftill works ouer. A great affecter of wits and fuch pretineffes; and his company is coftly to him, for he feldom ha's it but inuited. His friendfhip commonly is begun in a fupper and loft in lending money. The Tauerne is a dangerous place to him, for to drinke and to be drunke, is with him all one, and his braine is fooner quench'd then his thirft. He is drawn into naughtines with company, but fuffers alone, and the Baftard commonly laid to his charge. One that will bee patiently abus'd, and take exceptions a Moneth after when he vnderftands it, and then not [you cannot] endeare him more then by coozening him, and it is a temptation

to thofe that would not. One difcouerable in all filli-
neffes to all men but himfelfe, and you may take any
mans knowledge of him better then his owne. Hee
will promife the fame thing to twenty, and rather then
denie one, breake with all. One that ha's no power
o're himfelfe, o're his bufineffe, o're his friends: but a
prey and pitie to all: and if his fortunes once finke,
men quickly crie, Alas, and forget him.

38. *A Tobacco-feller*

IS the onely man that finds good in it which
others brag of, but doe not; for it is meate,
drinke, and clothes to him. No man opens
his ware with greater ferioufneffe, or chal-
lenges your iudgement more in the approbation. His Shop is the Randeuous of fpitting,
where men dialogue with their nofes, and their communication is fmoke. It is the place onely where
Spaine is commended, and prefer'd before England
it felfe. He fhould be wel experienc'd in the world:
for he ha's daily tryall of mens noftrils, and none is
better acquainted with humors. Hee is the piecing
commonly of fome other trade, which is bawd to his
Tobacco, and that to his wife, which is the flame that
followes this fmoke.

39. *A plaufible Man*

IS one that would faine run an euen path
in the world, and iutt againft no man. His
endeuour is not to offend, and his ayme
the generall opinion. His conuerfation is
a kind of continued Complement, and his
life practice of manners. The relation hee beares
to others, a kind of fafhionable refpect, not friendfhip,
but friendlines, which is equall to all and generall, and
his kindneffes feldome exceed courtefies. Hee loues
not deeper mutualities, becaufe he would not take
fides, nor hazard himfelfe on difpleafures, which he

principally auoids. At your firſt acquaintance with
him hee is exceeding kind and friendly, and at your
twentieth meeting after but friendly ſtill. He has an
excellent command ouer his patience and tongue,
eſpecially the laſt, which hee accommodates alwayes
to the times and perſons, and ſpeakes ſeldome what
is ſincere, but what is ciuill. He is one that vſes all
companies, drinkes all healths, and is reaſonable coole
in all Religons. He can liſten to a fooliſh diſcourſe
with an applauſiue attention, and conceale his Laughter at Non-ſenſe. Silly men much honour and eſteeme
him, becauſe by his faire reaſoning with them as with
men of vnderſtanding, he puts them into an erroneous
opinion of themſelues, and makes them forwarder
heereafter to their owne diſcouerie. Hee is one rather
well thought on then belou'd, and that loue he ha's,
is more of whole companies together then any one in
particular. Men gratifie him notwithſtanding with a
good report, and what-euer vices he ha's beſides, yet
hauing no enemies, he is ſure to be an honeſt fellow.

40. *The Worlds wiſe Man*

IS an able and ſufficient wicked man, it is
a proofe of his ſufficiency that hee is not
called wicked, but wiſe. A man wholy
determin'd in himſelfe and his owne ends,
and his inſtrument: herein any thing that
will doe it. His friends are a part of his engines, and
as they ſerue this worke, vs'd or laid by. Indeed hee
knowes not this thing of friend, but if hee giue you the
name, it is a ſigne he ha's a plot on you. Neuer more
actiue in his buſineſſes, then when they are mixt with
ſome harme to others: and tis his beſt play in this
Game to ſtrike off and lie in the place. Succeſsfull
commonly in theſe vndertakings, becauſe he paſſes
ſmoothly thoſe rubs which others ſtumble at, as Conſcience and the like: and gratulates himſelfe much in
this aduantage: Oathes and falſhood he counts the

neereſt way, and loues not by any meanes to goe
about. Hee has many fine quips at this folly of plaine
dealing, but his tuſh is greateſt at Religion, yet hee
vſes this too, and Vertue, and good Words, but is leſſe
dangerouſly a Diuel then a Saint. He aſcribes all
honeſtie to an vnpractis'dneſſe in the World: and
Conſcience a thing meerely for Children. Hee ſcornes
all that are ſo ſilly to truſt him, and onely not ſcornes
his enemie; eſpecially if as bad as himſelfe: He feares
him as a man well arm'd, and prouided, but ſets
boldly on good natures, as the moſt vanquiſhable.
One that ſeriouſly admires thoſe worſt Princes, as
Sforza, *Borgia*, and *Richard* the Third: and cals
matters of deepe villany things of difficultie. To
whom murders are but reſolute Acts, and Treaſon a
buſineſſe of great confequence. One whom two or
three Countries make vp to this compleatneſſe, and
he ha's traueld for the purpoſe. His deepeſt indear-
ment is a communication of miſchiefe, and then onely
you haue him faſt. His concluſion is commonly one
of theſe two, either a Great Man, or hang'd.

41. *A Bowle Alley*

IS the place where there are three things
throwne away beſide Bowls, to wit, time,
money and curſes, and the laſt ten for one.
The beſt Sport in it is the Gameſters,
and he enioyes it that lookes on and bets
not. It is the Schoole of wrangling, and worſe then
the Schooles, for men will cauill here for an haires
breadth, and make a ſtirre where a ſtraw would end the
controuerſie. No Anticke, ſcrewes mens bodies into
ſuch ſtrange flexures, and you would think them ſenſ-
leſſe, to ſpeak ſenſe to their Bowle, and put their truſt
in intreaties for a good caſt. The Betters are the
factious noiſe of the Alley, or the gameſters beads-
men that pray for them. They are ſomewhat like
thoſe that are cheated by great Men, for they loſe their

mony and muſt ſay nothing. It is the beſt diſcouery
of humors, eſpecially in the loſers, where you haue
fine variety of impatience, whilſt ſome fret, ſome raile,
ſome ſweare, and others more ridiculouſly comfort
themſelues with Philoſophy. To giue you the Morall
of it ; It is the Embleme of the world, or the worlds
ambition : where moſt are ſhort, or ouer, or wide or
wrong Byas't, and ſome few iuſtle in to the Miſtris Fortune. And it is here as in the Court, where the neareſt
are moſt ſpighted, and all blowes aym'd at the Toucher.

42. *A Surgeon*

IS one that has ſome buſineſſe about his
Building or little houſe of man, whereof
Nature is as it were the Tyler, and hee
the Playſterer. It is ofter out of reparations,
then an old Parſonage, and then he is ſet on
worke to patch it againe. Hee deales moſt with
broken Commodities, as a broken Head, or a mangled
face, and his gaines are very ill got, for he liues by the
hurts of the Common-wealth. He differs from a Phy-
ſitian as a ſore do's from a diſeaſe, or the ſicke from
thoſe that are not whole, the one diſtempers you
within, the other bliſters you without. He complaines
of the decay of Valour in theſe daies, and ſighes for
that flaſhing Age of Sword and Buckler ; and thinkes
the Law againſt Duels, was made meerly to wound his
Vocation. Hee had beene long ſince vndone, if the
charitie of the Stewes had not relieued him, from
whom he ha's his Tribute as duely as the Pope, or a
wind-fall ſometimes from a Tauerne, if a quart Pot
hit right. The rareneſſe of his cuſtome mak[e]s him
pittileſſe when it comes : and he holds a Patient
longer then our Courts a Cauſe. Hee tels you what
danger you had beene in if he had ſtaide but a
minute longer, and though it bee but a prickt finger,
hee makes of it much matter. He is a reaſonable
cleanely man, conſidering the Scabs hee ha's to deale

with, and your finest Ladies now and then are beholding to him for their best dressings. Hee curses old Gentlewomen, and their charity that mak[e]s his Trade their Almes: but his enuie is neuer stir'd so much as when Gentlemen goe ouer to fight vpon Calice Sands, whome hee wishes drown'd ere they come there, rather then the French shal get his Custome.

43. *A Shee precise Hypocrite*

IS one in whom good Women suffer, and haue their truth mis-interpreted by her folly. She is one, she knows not what her selfe if you aske her, but shee is indeed one that ha's taken a toy at the fashion of Religion, and is enamour'd of the New-fangle. Shee is a Nonconformist in a close Stomacher and Ruffle of Geneua Print, and her puritie consists much in her Linen. Shee ha's heard of the Rag of Rome, and thinkes it a very sluttish Religion, and rayles at the Whore of Babylon for a very naughty Woman. Shee ha's left her Virginity as a Relique of Popery, and marries in her Tribe without a Ring. Her deuotion at the Church is much in the turning vp of her eye, and turning downe the leafe in her Booke when shee heares nam'd Chapter and Verse. When she comes home, shee commends the Sermon for the Scripture, and two houres. She loues Preaching better then Praying, and of Preachers Lecturers, and thinkes the Weeke-dayes Exercise farre more edifying then the Sundaies. Her oftest Gossipings are Sabaoth-dayes iourneyes, where (though an enemy to Superstition) shee will goe in Pilgrimage fiue mile to a silenc'd Minister, when there is a better Sermon in her owne Parish. Shee doubts of the Virgin Marie's Saluation, and dare not Saint her, but knowes her owne place in heauen as perfectly, as the Pew shee ha's a key to. Shee is so taken vp with Faith, shee ha's no roome for Charity, and vnderstands no good

Workes, but what are wrought on the Sampler. She accounts nothing Vices but Superſtition, and an Oath, and thinkes Adultery a leſſe ſinne, then to ſweare by my Truely. Shee rayles at other Women by the names of *Iezabel* and *Dalilah* : and calls her owne daughters *Rebecka* and *Abigail,* and not *Anne* but *Hannah.* Shee ſuffers them not to learne on the Virginalls, becauſe of their affinity with the Organs, but is reconcil'd to the Bells for the Chymes ſake, ſince they were reform'd to the tune of a Pſalme. She ouer flowes ſo with the Bible, that ſhe ſpils it vpon euery occaſion, and wil not Cudgell her Maides without Scripture. It is a queſtion, whether ſhee is more troubled with the Diuell or the Diuell with her : ſhee is alwayes challenging and daring him, and her weapons are Spels no leſſe potent then different, as being the ſage Sentences of ſome of her owne Sectaries. No thing angers her ſo much as that Woemen cannot Preach, and in this point onely thinkes the Browniſt erroneous : but what ſhee cannot at the Church, ſhee do's at the Table, where ſhe prattles more then any againſt ſenſe, and Antichriſt, till a Capon wing ſilence her. Shee expounds the Prieſts of *Baal* Reading Miniſters, and thinkes the Saluation of that Pariſh as deſperate as the Turkes. Shee is a maine derider to her capacitie of thoſe that are not her Preachers, and cenſures all Sermons but bad ones. If her Husband be a Tradſman, ſhee helpes him to Cuſtomers, how ſoeuer to good cheere, and they are a moſt faithful couple at theſe meetings : for they neuer faile. Her Conſcience is like others Luſt neuer ſatisfied, and you might better anſwere *Scotus* then her Scruples. Shee is one that thinkes ſhee performes all her duty to God in hearing, and ſhewes the fruites of it in talking. Shee is more fiery againſt the May-pole then her Husband, and thinkes he might doe a Phinehas his act to break the pate of the Fiddler. She is an euerlaſting Argument ; but I am weary of her.

44. *A Contemplatiue Man*

IS a Scholler in this great Vniuerſity the World; and the ſame his Booke and Study. Hee cloyſters not his Meditations in the narrow darkneſſe of a Roome, but ſends them abroad with his Eyes, and his Braine trauels with his Feete. He looks vpon Man from a high Tower, and ſees him trulyer at this diſtance in his Infirmities and pooreneſſe. He ſcornes to mixe himſelfe in mens actions, as he would to act vpon a Stage; but ſits aloft on the Scaffold a cenſuring Spectator. Nature admits him as a partaker of her Sports, and asks his approbation as it were of her owne Workes, and variety. Hee comes not in Company, becauſe hee would not be ſolitary, but findes Diſcourſe enough with himſelfe, and his owne thoughts are his excellent play-fellowes. He lookes not vpon a thing as a yawning Stranger at nouelties: but his ſearch is more myſterious and inward, and hee ſpels Heauen out of earth. He knits his obſeruations together, and makes a Ladder of them all to climbe to God. He is free from vice, becauſe he has no occaſion to imploy it, and is aboue thoſe ends that make men wicked. He ha's learnt all can heere be taught him, and comes now to Heauen to ſee more.

45. *An Aturney.*

HIs Ancient beginning was a blue coat, ſince a liuery, and his hatching vnder a Law[y]er; whence though but pen-feather'd, hee hath now neſted for himſelfe, and with his horded pence purchaſt an Office. Two Deskes, and a quire of Paper ſet him vp, where he now ſits in ſtate for all commers. We can call him no great Author, yet he writes very much, and with the infamy of the Court is maintain'd in his

libels. Hee ha's fome fmatch of a Scholler, and yet
vfes Latine very hardly, and left it fhould accufe him,
cuts it off in the midft, and will not let it fpeake out.
He is contrary to great men, maintained by his fol-
lowers, that is his poore country Clients, that worfhip
him more then their Landlord, and be there neuer
fuch churles, he lookes for their curtefie. He firft
racks them foundly himfelfe, and then deliuers them
to the Lawier for execution. His looks are very foli-
citous importing much haft and difpatch, he is neuer
without his hanfull of bufineffe, that is, of paper. His
fkin becomes at laft as dry as parchment and his face
as intricate as the moft winding caufe. He talkes
Statutes as fiercely, as if he had mooted feuen yeers
in the Inns of Court; when all his skill is ftucke in
his girdle, or in his office window. Strife and wrangling haue made him rich, and he is thankfull to his
benefactor, and nourifhes it. If he liue in a Country
village, he makes all his neighbours good Subiects;
for there fhall be nothing done but what there is law
for. His bufineffe giues him not leaue to thinke of
his confcience, and when the time, or terme of his
life is going out, for Doomef-day he is fecure; for he
hopes he has a tricke to reuerfe iudgement.

46. *A Scepticke in Religion*

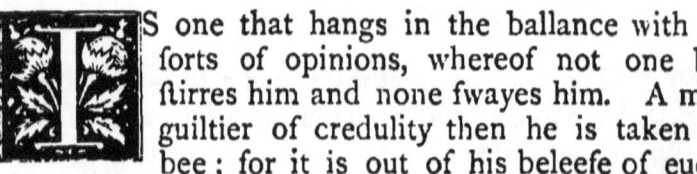S one that hangs in the ballance with all
forts of opinions, whereof not one but
ftirres him and none fwayes him. A man
guiltier of credulity then he is taken to
bee; for it is out of his beleefe of euery
thing, that hee fully beleeues nothing. Each Religion
fcarres him from it's contrary: none perfwades him to
it felfe. Hee would be wholy a Chriftian, but that he
is fomething of an Atheift. and wholy an Atheift, but
that hee is partly a Chriftian; and a perfect Here-
tick, but that there are fo many to diftract him. He

finds reafon in all opinions, truth in none : indeed the leaft reafon perplexes him, and the beft will not fatisfie him. He is at moft a confus'd and wild Chriftian, not fpecializ'd, by any forme, but capable of all. He vfes the Land's Religion, becaufe it is next him, yet hee fees not why hee may not take the other, but he chufes this, not as better, but becaufe there is not a pin to choofe. He finds doubts and fcruples better then refolues them, and is alwayes too hard for himfelfe. His Learning is too much for his brayne ; and his iudgment too little for his learning, and his oueropinion of both fpoyls all. Pity it was his mifchance of being a Scholler : for it do's only diftract and irregulate him and the world by him. He hammers much in generall vpon our opinions vncertainety, and the poffibility of erring makes him not venture on what is true. He is troubled at this naturalneffe of Religion to Countries, that Proteftantifme fhould bee borne fo in England and Popery abroad, and that fortune and the Starres fhould fo much fhare in it. Hee likes not this connexion of the Common-weale, and Diuinity, and feares it may be an Arch-practice of State. In our differences with Rome he is ftrangely vnfix't, and a new man euery day, as his laft difcourfebooks Meditations tranfport him. Hee could like the gray haires of Poperie, did not fome dotages their ftagger him ; hee would come to vs fooner, but our new name affrights him. He is taken with their Miracl[e]s but doubts an impufture ; hee conceiues of our Doctrine better but it feemes too empty and naked. He cannot driue into his fancy the circumfcription of Truth to our corner, and is as hardly perfwaded to thinke their old Legends true. He approues wel of our Faith, and more of their workes, and is fometimes much affected at the zeale of Amfterdam. His confcience interpofes, it felfe betwixt Duellers, and whillft it would part both, is by both wounded. He will fomtimes propend much to vs vpon the reading a good Writer, and at *Bellarmine* recoyles as farre backe

againe; and the Fathers iuſtle him from one ſide to
another. Now *Soſinaas* and *Vorſtius* afreſh torture
him, and he agrees with none worſe then himſelfe.
He puts his foot into Hereſies tenderly, as a Cat in
the water, and pulls it out againe, and ſtill ſomething
vnanſwer'd delayes him yet he beares away ſome parcell of each, and you may ſooner picke all Religions
out of him then one. He cannot thinke ſo many wiſe
men ſhould be in error, nor ſo many honeſt men out
of the way and his wounder is dubled, when he ſees
theſe oppoſe one annother. He hates authority as the
Tyrant of reaſon, and you cannot anger him worſe
then with a Fathers *dixit*, and yet that many are not
perſwaded with reaſon, ſhall authorize his doubt. In
ſumme, his whole life is a queſtion, and his ſaluation
a greater, which death onely concludes, and then he
is reſolu'd.

47. *A Partiall Man*

IS the oppoſite extreame to a Defamer, for
the one ſpeakes ill falſly, and the other well,
and both ſlander the Truth. He is one
that is ſtill weighing men in the Scale
of Compariſons, and puts his affection in
the one ballance and that ſwayes. His friend alwayes
ſhall doe beſt, and you ſhall rarely heare good of his
enemy. Hee conſiders firſt the man, and then the
thing, and reſtraines all merit to what they deſerue of
him. Commendations hee eſteemes not the debt of
Worth, but the requitall of kindneſſe: and if you aske
his reaſon, ſhewes his Intereſt and tels you how much
he is beholding to that Man. Hee is one that ties
his iudgement to the Wheele of Fortune, and they
determine giddily both alike. He preferres England
before other Countries, becauſe he was borne there,
and Oxford before other Vniuerſities, becauſe hee was
brought vp there, and the beſt Scholler there, is one
of his owne Colledge, and the beſt Scholler there is

one of his friends. Hee is a great fauourer of great perfons, and his argument is ftill that which fhould bee Antecedent, as he is in high place, therefore vertuous, he is prefer'd, therefore worthy. Neuer aske his opinion, for you fhall heare but his faction, and he is indifferent in nothing but Confcience. Men efteeme him for this a zealous affectionate, but they miftake him many times, for hee does it but to bee efteemed fo. Of all men hee is worft to write an Hiftorie, for hee will praife a *Seianus* or *Tiberius*, and for fome pettie refpect of his all pofteritie fhall bee cofen'd.

48. *A Trumpeter*

IS the Elephant with the great Trunke, for hee eates nothing but what comes through this way. His Profeffion is not fo worthy as to occafion infolence, and yet no man fo much puft vp. His face is as Brazen as his Trumpet, and (which his worfe) as a Fidlers, from whom hee differeth onely in this, that his impudence is dearer. The Sea of Drinke, and much wind make a Storme perpetually in his Cheeks, and his looke is like his noyfe, bluftering and tempeftuous. Hee wa's whilome the found of Warre, but now of Peace; yet as terrible as euer, for wherefoeuer hee comes they are fure to pay for't. He is the common attendant of glittering folkes, whether in the Court or Stage, where he is alwaies the Prologues Prologue. He is fomewhat in the nature of a Hogfhed fhrilleft when he is empty; when his belly is full hee is quiet enough. No man proues life more to bee a blaft, or himfelfe a bubble, and he is like a counterfeit Bankrupt, thriues beft when he is blowne vp.

49. *A vulgar-spirited Man*

IS one of the heard of the World. One that followes meerely the common crye, and makes it louder by one. A man that loues none but who are publikely affected, and he will not be wifer then the reſt of the Towne. That neuer ownes a friend after an ill name, or fome generall imputation though he knowes it moſt vnworthy. That oppofes to reafon, Thus men fay, and thus moſt doe, and thus the world goes, and thinkes this enough to poyfe the other. That worſhips men in place, and thofe onely, and thinkes all a great man fpeakes Oracles. Much taken with my Lords Ieſt, and repeats you it all to a fillable. One that iuſtifies nothing out of faſhion, nor any opinion out of the applauded way. That thinkes certainly all Spaniards and Iefuites very villaines, and is ſtill curfing the Pope and *Spynola*. One that thinkes the graueſt Caffocke the beſt Scholler: and the beſt Clothes the fineſt man. That is taken onely with broad and obfcœne wit, and hiffes any thing too deepe for him. That cries *Chaucer* for his Money aboue all our Engliſh Poets, becaufe the voice ha's gone fo, and hee ha's read none. That is much rauiſht with fuch a Noble mans courtefie, and would venture his life for him, becaufe he put off his Hat. One that is formoſt ſtill to kiffe the Kings hand, and cryes *God bleſſe his Maieſtie* loudeſt. That rayles on all men condemn'd and out of fauour, and the firſt that fayes away with the Traytors: yet ſtruck with much ruth at Executions, and for pittie to fee a man die, could kill the Hangman. That comes to London to fee it, and the pretty things in it, and the chiefe caufe of his iourney the Beares: That meafures the happineſſe of the Kingdome, by the cheapneſſe of corne; and conceiues no

harme of State, but il trading. Within this compaſſe
too, come thoſe that are too much wedg'd into the
world, and haue no lifting thoughts aboue thoſe things
that call to thriue, to doe well, and Preferment onely
the grace of God. That ayme all Studies at this
marke, and ſhew you poore Schollers as an example to
take heed by. That thinke the Priſon and want, a
Iudgement for ſome ſin, and neuer like well hereafter
of a Iayle-bird. That know no other Content but
wealth, brauery, and the Towne-Pleaſures; that thinke
all elſe but idle ſpeculation, and the Philoſophers,
mad-men: In ſhort, men that are carried away with all
outwardneſſes, ſhews, appearances, the ſtreame, the
people; for there is no man of worth but has a piece
of ſingularity, and ſcornes ſomething.

50. *A Herald*

IS the ſpawne, or indeed but the reſul-
tancie of Nobility, and to the making of
him went not a Generation, but a Genea-
logie. His Trade is Honour, and hee ſells
it, and giues Armes himſelfe, though hee
be no Gentleman. His bribes are like thoſe of a
corrupt Iudge; for they are the prices of blood. He
ſeemes very rich in diſcourſe, for he tels you of whole
fields of gold and ſiluer, Or and Argent, worth much
in French, but in Engliſh nothing. He is a great
diuer in the ſtreames or iſſues of Gentrie, and not a
by-Channell or baſtard eſcapes him, yet he dos with
them like ſome ſhameleſſe Queane, fathers more children on them, then euer they begot. His Trafficks is
a kind of Pedlery ware, Scutchions, and Pennons and
little Daggers, and Lyons, ſuch as Children eſteeme
and Gentlemen: but his peni-worths are rampant, for
you may buy three whole Brawns cheaper, then three
Boars heads of him painted. Hee was ſomtimes
the terrible Coat of *Mars*, but is now for more
mercifull Battels in the Tilt-yard, where whoſoeuer

is victorious, the spoiles are his. Hee is an Art in
England, but in Wales Nature, where they are
borne with Heraldry in their mouthes, and each
Name is a Pedegree.

51. *A Plodding Student*

IS a kind of Alchymiſt or Perſecuter of Nature, that would change the dull lead of his
Brain into finer mettle, with ſucceſſe many
times as vnproſperous, or at leaſt not
quitting the coſt, to wit, of his own Oyle
and Candles. He ha's a ſtrange forc't appetite to
Learning, and to atchieue it brings nothing but patience
and a body. His Studie is not great but continuall,
and conſiſts much in the ſitting vp till after Midnight
in a rug-gowne, and a Night cap to the vanquiſhing
perhaps of ſome ſixe lines: yet what hee ha's, he ha's
perfect, for he reads it ſo long to vnderſtand it till he
gets it without Booke. Hee may with much induſtry
make a breach into Logicke, and ariue at ſome ability
in an Argument: but for politer Studies hee dare not
skirmiſh with them, and for Poetry accounts it im-
pregnable. His Inuention is no more then the finding
out of his Papers, and his few gleanings there, and
his diſpoſition of them is as iuſt as the Book-binders,
a ſetting or glewing of them together. Hee is a great
diſcomforter of young Students, by telling them what
trauell it ha's coſt him, and how often his braine
turn'd at Philoſophy, and makes others feare Studying
as a cauſe of Duncery. Hee is a man much giuen to
Apothegms which ſerue him for wit, and ſeldome
breakes any Ieſt, but which belong'd to ſome Lace-
demonian or Romane in *Lycoſthenes*. He is like a dull
Cariers horſe, that will go a whole weeke together but
neuer out of a foot-pace: and hee that ſets forth on
the Saturday ſhall ouertake him.

52. *Pauls Walke*

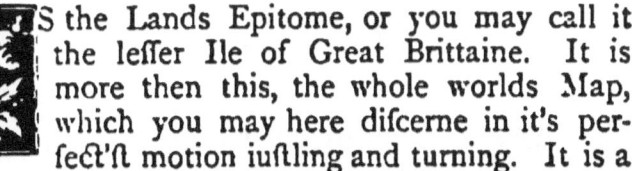S the Lands Epitome, or you may call it the leſſer Ile of Great Brittaine. It is more then this, the whole worlds Map, which you may here diſcerne in it's perfect'ſt motion iuſtling and turning. It is a heape of ſtones and men, with a vaſt confuſion of Languages and were the Steeple not ſanctified nothing liker Babel. The noyſe in it is like that of Bees, a ſtrange humming or buzze-mixt of walking, tongues and feet: It is a kind of ſtill roare or loud whiſper. It is the great Exchange of all diſcourſe, and no buſines whatſoeuer but is here ſtirring and afoot. It is the Synod of all pates politicke, ioynted and laid together in moſt ſerious poſture, and they are not halfe ſo buſie at the Parliament. It is the Anticke of tailes to tailes, and backes to backes, and for vizards you need goe no further then faces. It is the Market of young Lecturers, whom you may cheapen here at all rates and ſizes. It is the generall Mint of all famous lies, which are here like the legands Popery, firſt coyn'd and ſtampt in the Church. All inuentions are emptyed here, and not few pockets. The beſt ſigne of a Temple in it is, that it is the Theeues Sanctuary, which robbe more ſafely in the Croud, then a wilderneſſe, whilſt euery ſearcher is a buſh to hide them. It is the other expence of the day, after Playes, Tauerne, and a Baudy-Houſe, and men haue ſtill ſome Oathes left to ſweare here. It is the eares Brothell, and ſatisfies their luſt, and ytch. The Viſitants are all men without exceptions, but the principall Inhabitants and poſſeſſors, are ſtale Knights, and Captaines out of Seruice, men of long Rapiers, and Breeches, which after all turne Merchants here, and trafficke for Newes. Some make it a Preface to their Dinner, and Trauell for a Stomacke: but thriftier men make it their Ordinarie: and Boord here verie cheape. Of all ſuch places it is leaſt haunted with Hobgoblins, for if a Ghoſt would walke more, hee could not.

53. *A Vniuerſitie Dunne*

IS a Gentlemans follower cheaply purchas'd, for his own money ha's hyred him. Hee is an inferiour Creditour of ſome ten ſhillings or downwards, contracted for Horſehire, or perchance for drinke, to weake to bee put in Suite. and he arreſts your modeſtie. Hee is now very expenſiue of his time, for hee will waite vpon your Staires a whole Afternoone, and dance attendance with more patience then a Gentleman-Vſher. Hee is a ſore beleaguerer of Chambers, and aſſaults them ſometimes with furious knockes: yet finds ſtrong reſiſtance commonly, and is kept out. Hee is a great complayner of Schollers loytering, for hee is ſure neuer to find them within, and yet hee is the chiefe cauſe many times that makes them ſtudie. He Grumbles at the ingratitude of men, that ſhunne him for his kindneſſe, but indeed it is his owne fault, for hee is too great an vpbrayder. No man put[s] them more to their braine then hee: and by ſhifting him off they learne to ſhift in the world. Some chooſe their roomes a purpoſe to auoide his ſurprizals, and thinke the beſt commoditie in them his Proſpect. Hee is like a reiected acquaintance, hunts thoſe that care not for his company, and hee knowes it well enough; and yet will not keepe away. The ſole place to ſupply him is the Butterie, where hee takes grieuous vſe vpon your Name, and hee is one much wrought with good Beere and Rhetoricke. He is a man of moſt vnfortunate voyages, and no Gallant walkes the ſtreet to leſſe purpoſe.

54. *A stayed Man*

S a man. One that ha's taken order with himselfe, and set a rule to those lawlesnesses within him. Whose life is distinct and in Method, and his Actions as it were cast vp before. Not loos'd into the Worlds vanities, but gathered vp and contracted in his station. Not scatter'd into many pieces of businesses, but that one course he takes, goes thorough with. A man firme and standing in his purposes, nor heau'd off with each wind and passion. That squares his expence to his Coffers, and makes the Totall first, and then the Items. One that thinkes what hee does, and does what he sayes, and forsees what he may doe, before he purposes. One whose (if I can) is more then anothers assurance, and his doubtfull tale before some mens protestations. That is confident of nothing in futurity, yet his coniectures oft true Prophecies. That makes a pause still betwixt his eare and beleefe, and is not too hasty to say after others : One whose Tongue is strung vp like a Clocke till the time, and then strikes, and sayes much when hee talkes little. That can see the Truth betwixt two wranglers, and sees them agree euen in that they fall out vpon. That speakes no Rebellion in a brauery, or talkes bigge from the spirit of Sacke. A man coole and temperate in his passions, not easily betraid by his choller : That vies not oath with oath, nor heat with heat : but replies calmly to an angry man, and is too hard for him too. That can come fairely off from Captaines companies, and neither drink nor quarrell. One whom no ill hunting sends home discontented, and makes him sweare at his dogs and family. One not hastie to pursue the new Fashion, nor yet affectedly true to his old round Breeches. But grauely handsome, and to his place, which suites him better then his Tailor. Actiue in the world without disquiet, and carefull without miserie : yet neither

ingulft in his pleafures, nor a feeker of bufineffe, but ha's his houres for both. A man that feldome laughes violently, but his mirth is a cheerefull looke. Of a compos'd and fetled countenance, not fet, nor much alterable with fadneffe or ioy. He affects nothing fo wholy, that hee muft bee a miferable man when he lofes it: but forethinks what will come hereafter, and ipares Fortune his thanks and curfes. One that louse his Credit, not this word Reputation; yet can faue both without a Duell: whofe entertainments to greater men are refpectfull not complementary, and to his friends plaine not rude. A good Husband, Father, Mafter: that is without doting, pampring, familiarity. A man well poys'd in all humours in whom Nature fhewed moft Geometry, and hee ha's not fpoyl'd the worke. A man of more wifedome then wittineffe, and braine then fancy; and abler to any thing then to make Verfes.

FINIS.

Micro-cosmographie.

Additional Characters.

Twenty-three first found in
Fifth Edition, 1629.

One firſt found in
Sixth Edition, 1633.

[CHARACTERS FIRST FOUND IN FIFTH EDITION, 1629.]

55. *A modeſt man*

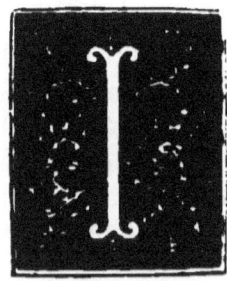

IS a far finer man then he knowes of, one that ſhewes better to all men then him ſelfe, and ſo much the better to al men, as leſſe to himſelfe: for no quality ſets a man off like this, and commends him more againſt his will: And he can put vp any iniury ſooner then this, (as he tells it) your Ironie. You ſhall heare him confute his commenders, and giuing reaſons how much they are miſtaken, and is angry almoſt, if they do not beleeue him. Nothing threatens him ſo much as great expectation, which he thinks more prejudiciall, then your vnder-opinion, becauſe it is eaſier to make that falſe; then this true. He is one that ſneaks from a good action, as one that had pilferd, and dare not iuſtifie it, and is more bluſhingly deprehended in this, then others in ſin. That counts al publike declarings of himſelfe, but ſo many penances before the people, and the more you applaud him, the more you abaſh him, and he recouers not his face a moneth after. One that is eaſie to like any thing, of another mans, and thinkes all hee knowes not of him better, then that he knowes. He excuſes that to you, which another would impute, and if you pardon him, is ſatisfied. One that ſtands in no opinion becauſe it is his owne, but ſuſpects it rather, becauſe it is his owne, and is confuted, and thankes you. Hee ſees nothing more willingly then his errors; and it is his error ſometimes to be too ſoone perſwaded. He is content to be Auditor, where he only can ſpeake, and content to goe away, and thinke himſelfe inſtructed. No man is ſo weake that he is aſhamed to learne of, and is leſſe aſhamed to confeſſe it: and he

finds many times in the duſt, what others ouerlooke,
and loſe. Euery mans preſence is a kinde of bridle to
him, to ſtop the rouing of his tongue and paſſions:
and euen impudent men looke for their reuerence from
him, and diſtaſte that in him, which they ſuffer in
themſelues, as one in whom vice is ill-fauoured, and
ſhewes more ſcuruily then another. A bawdy ieſt
ſhall ſhame him more then a baſtard another man, and
he that got it, ſhall cenſure him among the reſt. And
hee is coward to nothing more then an ill tongue, and
whoſoeuer dare lye on him hath power ouer him, and
if you take him by his looke, he is guilty. The maine
ambition of his life is not to be diſcredited: and for
other things, his deſires are more limited then his fortunes, which he thinkes preferment though neuer ſo
meane, and that he is to doe ſomething to deſerue
this: Hee is too tender to venter on great places, and
would not hurt a dignity to helpe himſelfe. If he doe,
it was the violence of his friends conſtraind him, and
how hardly ſoeuer hee obtaine it, he was harder perſwaded to ſeeke it.

56. *A meere emptie wit*

IS like one that ſpends on the ſtocke without
any reuenues comming in, and will ſhortly
be no wit at al: for learning is the fuell
to this fire of wit, which if it wants this
feeding, eates out it ſelfe. A good conceit or two bates of ſuch a man, and makes a ſenſible
weakning in him: and his braine recouers it not a
yeere after. The reſt of him are bubbles and flaſhes
darted out on the ſudden, which if you take them
while they are warme, may be laught at; if they coole,
are nothing. He ſpeakes beſt on the preſent appre-
henſion, for meditation ſtupifies him, and the more he
is in trauell, the leſſe he brings forth. His things
come off then, as in a nauſeating ſtomacke, where
there is nothing to caſt vp ſtraines, and convulſions,

and fome aftonifhing bumbaft which men onely, till
they vnderftand, are fcar'd with. A verfe or fome fuch
worke he may fometimes get vp to, but feldome aboue
the ftature of an Epigram, and that with fome reliefe
out of Martial, which is the ordinary companion of
his pocket, and he reades him as he were infpir'd.
Such men are commonly the trifling things of the
world, good to make merry the companie, and whom
only men haue to doe withall, when they haue nothing
to doe, and none are leffe their friends, then who are
moft their companie. Here they vent themfelues o're
a cup fomewhat more laftingly, all their words goe
for iefts, and all their iefts for nothing. They are
nimble in the fancy of fome ridiculous thing, and
reafonable good in the expreffion. Nothing ftops a
ieft when it is comming, neither friends, nor danger,
but it muft out howfoeuer, though their blood come
out after, and then they emphatically raile, and are
emphatically beaten, and commonly are men reafonable familiar to this. Briefely they are fuch whofe
life is but to laugh, and be laught at:.and onely wits
in ieft, and fooles in earneft.

57. *A Drunkard*

IS one that will be a man to morrow morn-
ing: but is now what you will make him,
for he is in the power of the next man,
and if a friend, the better. One that
hath let goe himfelfe from the hold and ftay
of reafon, and lyes open to the mercie of all temptations.
No luft but findes him difarm[e]d and fenceleffe, and with
the leaft affault enters: if any mifchiefe efcape him,
it was not his fault, for he was laid as faire for it, as
he could. Euery man fees him, as *Cham* faw his
father the firft of this finne, an *uncouer'd man*, and
though his garment bee on, vncouer'd: the fecreteft
parts of his foule lying in the nakedft manner vifible:
all his paffions come out now, all his vanities, and

those shamefuller humors which discretion clothes. His body becomes at last like a myrie way, where the spirits are to be-clog'd and cannot passe: all his members are out of office, and his heeles doe but trip vp one another. He is a blind man with eyes, and a cripple with legs on. All the vse he has of this vessell himselfe, is to hold thus much: for his drinking is but a scooping in of so many quarts, which are filld out into his bodie, and that fild out again into the Roome, which is commonly as drunke as hee. Tobacco serues to aire him after a washing, and is his onely breath, and breathing while. Hee is the greatest enemy to himselfe, and the next to his friend, and then most in the act of his kindnesse, for his kindnesse is but trying a mastery, who shall sinke down first: And men come from him as from a battel, wounded, and bound vp. Nothing takes a man off more from his credit, and businesse, and makes him more retchlesly carelesse, what becomes of all. Indeed hee dares not enter on a serious thought, or if hee doe, it is such melancholie, that it sends him to be drunke againe.

58. *A Prison*

IS the graue of the liuing, where they are shut vp from the world, and their friends: and the wormes that gnaw vpon them, their owne thoughts, and the Iaylor. A house of meager lookes, and ill smells: for lice, drink, Tobacco are the compound; Pluto's Court was express't from this fancy. And the persons are much about the same parity that is there. You may aske as *Menippus* in *Lucian*, which is *Nireus*, which *Thersites*, which the begger, which the Knight: for they [are] all suited in the same forme of a kinde of nastie pouerty. Onely to be out at elbowes is in fashion here, and a great Indecorum, not to be thredbare Euery man showes here like so many wracks vpon the Sea, here the ribs of a thoufand pound, here the relicke of fo many Mannours, a doublet without buttons. And tis a fpectacle of more pitty then executions are. The company one with other, is but a vying of complaints, and the caufes they haue, to rayle on fortune, and foole themfelues, and there is a great deale of good fellowfhip in this. They are commonly, next their Creditors, moft bitter againft the Lawyers, as men that haue had a great ftroke in affifting them hither. Mirth here is ftupidity or hardhartednes, yet they faine it fometimes to flip Melancholy and keep off themfelues from themfelues, and the torment of thinking what they haue beene. Men huddle vp their life here as a thing of no vfe, and weare it out like an old fuite, the fafter the better; and hee that deceiues the time beft, beft fpends it. It is the place where new commers are moft welcom'd, and next them ill newes, as that which extends their fellowfhip in mifery, and leaues fewer to infult: And they breathe their difcontents more fecurely here, and haue their tongues at more liberty then abroad. Men fee here much fin, and much calamity: and where the laft does not mortifie, the other hardens, and thofe that are worfe here, are defperately worfe, as thofe from whom the horror of finne is taken off, and the punifhment familiar. And commonly a hard thought paffes on all, that come from this Schoole: which though it teach much wifedome, it is too late, and with danger: and it is better bee a foole, then come here to learne it.

59. *A Seruingman*

IS one of the makings vp of a Gentleman, as well as his clothes: and fomewhat in the fame nature, for hee is caft behind his mafter as fafhionably as his fword and cloake are, and he is but *in querpo* without him. His properneffe qualifies him, and of that a good legge; for his head hee ha's little vfe but to keep it bare. A good dull wit beſt ſuits with him, to comprehend common ſence, and a trencher: for any greater store of braine it makes him but tumultuous, and ſeldome thriues with him. He followes his maſters ſteps, as well in conditions as the ſtreet: if he wench or drink, he comes after in an vnderkind, and thinkes it a part of his dutie to be like him. He is indeed wholly his maſters; of his faction, of his cut, of his pleaſures; hee is handſome for his credit, and drunke for his credit; and if hee haue power in the ſeller, commands the pariſh. He is one that keeps the beſt companie and is none of it; for he knowes all the Gentlemen his maſter knowes, and pick[e]s from them ſome Hawking, and horſe-race termes, which he ſwaggers with in the Ale-houſe, where he is onely called maſter. His mirth is baudie ieſts with the wenches, and behind the doore, bawdie earneſt. The beſt worke he does is his marrying, for it makes an honeſt woman, and if he follow in it his maſters direction, it is commonly the beſt ſeruice he does him.

60. *An Inſolent man*

IS a fellow newly great, and newly proud: one that ha's put himſelfe into another face vpon his preferment, for his owne was not bred to it. One whom fortune hath ſhot vp to ſome Office or Authority, and he ſhootes vp his necke to his fortune, and will not bate you an inch of either. His very countenance and geſture beſpeak how much he is, and if you vnderſtand him not, hee tels you, and concludes euery Period with his place, which you muſt and ſhall know. He is one that lookes on all men as if he were very angry, but eſpecially on thoſe of his acquaintance, whom hee beates off with a ſurlier diſtance, as men apt to miſtake him, becauſe they haue knowne him. And for this cauſe *he knowes not you, till you haue told him your name, which he thinkes hee has heard, but forgot,*

and with much adoe feemes to recouer. If you haue any
thing to vfe him in, you are his vaffal for that time,
and muft giue him the patience of an iniury, which hee
does only to fhew what he may doe. He fnaps you
vp bitterly, becaufe he will be offended, and tells you
you are fawcy and troublefom, and fometimes takes
your money in this language. His very courtefies
are intolerable, they are done with fuch arrogance and
imputation, and he is the onely man you may hate
after a good turne, and not bee vngratefull, and men
reckon it among their calamities to be beholding vnto
him. No vice drawes with it a more generall hoftility,
and makes men readier to fearch into his faults, and
of them, his beginning: and no tale fo vnlikely but
is willingly heard of him, and beleeu'd. And commonly fuch men are of no merit at all: but make out
in pride what they want in worth, and fence themfelues
with a ftately kinde of behauiour from that contempt
would purfue them. They are men whofe preferment
does vs a great deale of wrong, and when they are
downe, wee may laugh at them, without breach of
good Nature.

61. *Acquaintance*

IS the firft draught of a friend, whom we
muft lay downe oft thus, as the foule coppy,
before we can write him perfit, and true;
for from hence, as from a probation, men
take a degree in our refpect, till at
laft they wholly poffeffe vs. For acquaintance is the
heard, and friendfhip the paire chofen out of it; by
which at laft we begin to impropriate, and enclofe
to our felues, what before lay in common with
others. And commonly where it growes not vp to
this, it falls as low as may be: and no poorer relation
then old acquaintance, of whom we aske onely how
they doe for fafhion fake and care not. The ordinarie
vfe of acquaintance is but fomwhat a more boldneffe

of fociety, a fharing of talke, newes, drinke, mirth
together: but forrow is the right of a friend, as a thing
neerer our heart, and to be deliuer'd with it. Nothing
eafier then to create Acquaintance: the meere being
in company once, doe's it; whereas friendfhip like
children is ingendred by a more inward mixture, and
coupling together: when we are acquainted not with
their vertues onely, but their faults to, their paffions,
their feares, their fhame, and are bold on both fides to
make their difcouery. And as it is in the loue of the
body, which is then at the height and full, when it has
power and admittance into the hidden and worft parts
of it: So it is in friendfhip with the mind, when thofe
verenda of the foule, and thofe things which wee dare
not fhew the world, are bare and detected one to
another. Some men are familiar with all, and thofe
commonly friends to none: for friendfhip is a fullener
thing, as a contracter and taker vp of our affections
to fome few, and fuffers them not loofly to be fcatter'd
on all men. The pooreft tye of acquaintance is that
of place and countrie; which are fhifted as the place,
and mift but while the fancy of that continues. Thefe
are onely then gladdeft of other, when they meet in
fome forren region, where the encompaffing of ftrangers
vnites them clofer, till at laft they get new, and
throw off one another. Men of parts and eminencie
as their acquaintance is more fought for, fo they are
generally more ftaunch of it, not out of pride onely,
but feare to let too many in too neer them: for it is
with men as with pictures, the beft fhow better a
far off and at diftance; and the clofer you come to
them, the courfer they are. The beft iudgement of a
man, is taken from his Acquaintance; for friends and
enemies are both partiall; whereas thefe fee him trueft,
becaufe calmelieft, and are no way fo engag'd to lye for
him. And men that grow ftrange after acquaintance,
feldome peece together againe, as thofe that haue
tafted meat and diflike it, out of a mutuall experience
direllifhing one another.

62. A meere Complementall Man

IS one to be held off ſtill at the ſame diſtance you are now; for you ſhal haue him but thus, and if you enter on him further, you loſe him. Methinkes Virgil well expreſſes him in thoſe well-behau'd ghoſts that Æneas mette with, [that were] friends to talke with, and men to looke on, but if hee graſpt them, but ayre. He is one that lyes kindly to you, and for good faſhion ſake, and tis diſcourteſie in you to beleeue him. His words are but ſo many fine phraſes ſet together, which ſerue equally for all men, and are equally to no purpoſe. Each freſh encounter with a man, puts him to the ſame part againe, and he goes ouer to you; what hee ſaid to him was laſt with him. *Hee kiſſes your hands as hee kiſt his before, and is your ſeruant to bee commanded, but you ſhall entreat of him nothing.* His proffers are vniuerſall and generall with exceptions againſt all particulars; hee will doe any thing for you: but if you vrge him to this, hee cannot, or to that, he is engag'd: but hee will doe any thing. Promiſes he accounts but a kinde of mannerly words, and in the expectation of your manners, not to exact them, if you doe, hee wonders at your ill breeding, that cannot diſtinguiſh betwixt what is ſpoken and what is meant: No man giues better ſatisfaction at the firſt, and comes off more with the Elogie of a kind Gentleman, till you know him better, and then you know him for nothing. And commonly thoſe moſt raile at him, that haue before moſt commended him. The beſt is, hee coozens you in a faire manner, and abuſes you with great reſpect.

63. A poore Fidler

IS a man and a fiddle out of caſe: and he in worſe caſe then his fiddle. One that rubs two ſticks together, (as the Indians ſtrike fire) and rubs a poore liuing out of it: Partly from this, and partly from your

charity, which is more in the hearing, then giuing him,
for he fells nothing dearer then to be gone: He is
iuſt ſo many ſtrings aboue a begger, though he haue
but two: and yet hee begs too, onely not in the downe-
right *for Gods ſake, but with a ſhrugging God bleſſe
you*, and his face is more pyn'd than the blind mans.
Hunger is the greateſt paine he takes, except a broken
head ſometimes, and the labouring *Iohn Dorry*.
Otherwiſe his life is ſo many fits of mirth, and 'tis
ſome mirth to ſee him. A good feaſt ſhall draw him
fiue miles by the noſe, and you ſhall track him againe by
the ſent. His other Pilgrimages are Faires, and good
Houſes, where his deuotion is great to the Chriſtmas:
and no man loues good times better. Hee is in league
with the Tapſters for the worſhipfull of the Inne,
whom he torments next morning with his art, and ha's
their names more perfit then their men. A new ſong
is better to him then a new Iacket: especially if bawdie,
which hee calls merry, and hates naturally the Puritan,
as an enemy to this mirth. A countrey wedding, and
Whitſon ale are the two maine places he dominiers in,
where he goes for a Muſician, and over-look[es] the
Bag-pipe. The reſt of him is drunke, and in the
ſtocks.

64. *A medling man*

IS one that has nothing to do with his
buſineſſe, and yet no man buſier then
hee, and his buſineſſe is moſt in his face.
He is one thruſts himſelfe violently into
all employments, vnſent for, vn-fee'd, and
many times vn-thank't, and his part in it is onely an
eager buſtling, that rather keepes adoe, then do's any
thing. He will take you aſide, and queſtion you of your
affaire, and liſten with both eares, and looke earneſtly:
and then it is nothing ſo much yours as his. Hee
ſnatches what you are doing out of your hands, and
cryes *Giue it me*, and does it worſe, and layes an en-

gagement vpon you too, and you muſt thanke him for this paines. Hee layes you downe a hundred wild plots, all impoſſible things, which you muſt be ruled by perforce, and hee deliuers them with a ſerious and counſelling forehead, and there is a great deale more wiſedome in this forehead, then his head: Hee will woo for you, ſollicite for you, and woo you to ſuffer him: and ſcarce any thing done, wherein his letter, or his iourney, or at leaſt himſelfe is not ſeen: if he haue no taske in it elſe, he will raile yet on ſome ſide, and is often beaten when he neede not. Such men neuer thorowly weigh any buſineſſe, but are forward onely to ſhew their zeale, when many times this forwardneſſe ſpoiles it, and then they crie they haue done what they can, that is as much hurt. Wiſe men ſtill deprecate theſe mens kindneſſes, and are beholding to them rather to let them alone; as being one trouble more in all buſineſſe, and which a man ſhall be hardeſt rid of.

65. *A good old Man*

IS the beſt Antiquitie, and which we may with leaſt vanitie admire. One whom Time hath beene thus long a working, and like winter fruit ripen'd when others are ſhaken downe. He hath taken out as many leſſons of the world, as dayes, and learn't the beſt thing in it, the vanitie of it. Hee lookes o're his former life as a danger well paſt, and would not hazard himſelfe to begin againe. His luſt was long broken before his bodie, yet he is glad this temptation is broke too, and that hee is fortified from it by this weakeneſſe. The next doore of death ſads him not, but hee expects it calmely as his turne in Nature: and feares more his recoyling backe to childiſhnes then duſt. All men looke on him as a common father, and on old age for his ſake, as a reuerent thing. His very preſence, and face puts vice out of countenance, and makes it an indecorum in a vicious man. Hee practiſes his ex-

perience on youth without the harſhneſſe of reproofe,
and in his counfell is good companie. He ha's fome
old ſtories ſtill of his owne feeing to confirme what he
fayes, and makes them better in the telling; yet is not
troublefome neither with the fame tale againe, but
remembers with them, how oft he ha's told them. His
old fayings and moralls seeme proper to his beard:
and the poetrie of *Cato* do's well out of his mouth,
and hee fpeakes it as if he were the Author. Hee is
is not apt to put the boy on a yonger man, nor the foole
on a boy, but can diſtinguiſh grauity from a fowre
looke, and the leſſe teſtie he is, the more regarded.
You muſt pardon him if he like his own times better
than thefe, becaufe thofe things are follies to him now
that were wifedome then : yet he makes vs of that
opinion too, when we fee him, and coniecture thofe
times by fo good a Relicke. He is a man capable of
a deareneſſe with the yo[u]ngeſt men ; yet he not youth-
fuller for them, but they older for him, and no man
credits more his acquaintance. He goes away at leaſt
[laſt] too foone whenfoeuer, with all mens forrow but
his owne, and his memory is freſh, when it is twice
as old.

66. *A Flatterer*

IS the picture of a friend, and as pictures
flatter manie times, fo hee oft ſhewes fairer
then the true fubſtance : His looke, conuerfation, companie, and all the outward-
nes of friendſhippe more pleafing by odds,
for a true friend dare take the liberty to bee fometimes
offenfiue, whereas he is a great deale more cowardly,
and will not let the leaſt hold goe, for feare of lofing
you. Your meere fowre looke affrights him, and
makes him doubt his caſheering. And this is one fure
marke of him, that he is neuer firſt angry, but ready,
though vpon his owne wrong, to make fatisfaction.
Therefore hee is never yok't with a poore man or any

that ſtands on the lower ground, but whoſe fortunes
may tempt his pain͡e͡s to deceiue him. Him hee
learnes firſt, and learnes well, and growes perfitter in
his humours, then himſelfe, and by this doore enters
vpon his Soule: of which hee is able at laſt to take the
very print and marke, and faſhion his own by it like a
falſe key to open all your ſecrets. All his affections
iumpe euen with yours: hee is beforehand with your
thoughts, and able to ſuggeſt them vnto you. He will
commend to you firſt, what hee knowes you like, and
has alwayes ſome abſurd ſtory or other of your enemie,
and then wonders how your two opinions ſhould iumpe
in that man. Hee will aske your counſell ſometimes as
a man of deepe iudgement, and has a ſecret of purpoſe
to diſcloſe you, and whatſoeuer you ſay, is perſwaded.
Hee liſtens to your words with great attention, and
ſometimes will object that you may confute him, and
then proteſts hee neuer heard ſo much before. A
piece of witte burſts him with an ouerflowing laughter,
and hee remembers it for you to all companies, and
laughs againe in the telling. He is one neuer chides
you but for your vertues, as, *You are too good, too
honeſt, too religious*; when his chiding may ſeeme but
the earneſter commendation, and yet would faine
chide you out of them too: for your vice is the thing
he has vſe of, and wherein you may beſt vſe him, and
hee is neuer more actiue then in the worſt diligences.
Thus at laſt he poſſeſſes you from your ſelfe, and then
expects but his hyre to betray you. And it is a happineſſe not to diſcouer him; for as long as you are
happy, you ſhall not.

67. *A high ſpirited man*

S one that lookes like a proud man, but
is not: you may forgiue him his lookes
for his worth ſake, for they are only too
proud to be baſe. One whom no rate
can buy off from the leaſt piece of his

freedome, and makes him digeſt an vnworthy thought an houre. Hee cannot crouch to a great man to poſſeſſe him, nor fall low to the earth, to rebound neuer ſo high againe. Hee ſtands taller on his owne bottome, then others on the aduantage ground of fortune, as hauing ſolidly that honour, of which Title is but the pompe. Hee does homage to no man for his Great ſtyles ſake, but is ſtrictly iuſt in the exaction of reſpect againe, and will not bate you a Complement. He is more ſenſible of a neglect then an vndoing, and ſcornes no man ſo much as his ſurly threatner. A man quickly fired, and quickly laid downe with ſatisfaction, but remits any injury ſooner then words. Onely to himſelfe he is irreconcileable, whom hee neuer forgives a diſgrace, but is ſtill ſtabbing himſelfe with the thought of it, and no diſeaſe that he dyes of ſooner. Hee is one had rather pinch [periſh], then bee beholding for his life, and ſtriues more to bee quitte with his friend then his enemy. Fortune may kill him, but not deiect him, nor make him fall into a[n] humbler key then before, but he is now loftier then euer in his owne defence, you ſhall heare him talke ſtill after thouſands ; and he becomes it better, then thoſe that haue it. One that is aboue the world and its drudgery, and cannot pull downe his thoughts to the pelting buſineſſes of it [life]. He would ſooner accept the Gallowes then a meane trade, or any thing that might diſparage the height of man in him, and yet thinkes no death comparably baſe to hanging neither. One that will doe nothing vpon commaund, though hee would doe it otherwiſe : and if euer hee doe euill, it is when hee is dar'd to it. Hee is one that if fortune equal his worth, puts a luſter in all preferment, but if otherwiſe hee be too much croſt, turnes deſperately melancholy, and ſcornes mankind.

68. *A Meere Gull Citizen*

IS one much about the fame modell, and pitch of braine that the Clowne is, onely of fomewhat a more polite, and fynicall Ignorance, and as fillily fcornes him, as he is fillily admir'd by him. The quality of the Citty hath affoorded him fome better dreffes of clothes and language, which he vfes to the beft aduantage, and is fo much the more ridiculous. His chiefe education is the vifits of his Shop, where if Courtiers, and fine Ladies refort, hee is infected with fo much more eloquence, and if hee catch one word extraordinary, weares it for euer. You fhal heare him mince a complement fometimes that was neuer made for him: and no man payes dearer for good words, for he is oft payed with them. He is futed rather fine, then in the fafhion, and has ftill fomething to diftinguifh him from a Gentleman, though his doublet coft more: efpecially on Sundaies, Bride-groome-like, where he carries the ftate of a verie folemne man, and keepes his pew as his Shop: and it is a great part of his deuotion, to feaft the Minifter. But his chiefeft gueft is a cuftomer, which is the greateft relation hee acknowledges; efpecially if you be an honeft Gentleman, that is, truft him to coozen you enough. His friendfhips are a kinde of Goffiping friendfhips, and thofe commonly within the circle of his Trade, wherein he is carefull principally to auoid two things, that is, poore men, and furety-fhips. [He is] A man that will fpend his fixe pence with a great deale of imputation, and no man makes more of a pinte of wine then he. He is one beares a pretty kind of foolifh loue to Schollers, and to Cambridge efpecially for Sturbridges Faires fake: and of thefe all are trewants to him that are not preachers, and of thefe the lowdeft the beft: and he is *much rauifht with the noyfe of a rolling tongue.* He loues to heare difcourfes

out of his Element, and the leſſe he vnderſtands, the
better pleaſ'd, which he expreſſes in a ſmile, and ſome
fond Proteſtation. One that do's nothing without
his chuck, that is, his wife, with whom hee is billing
ſtill in conſpiracy, and the wantoner ſhe is, the more
power ſhe has ouer him: And ſhee neuer ſtoopes ſo
low after him, but is the onely woman goes better of
a widdow then a maid. In the education of his
child no man fearefuller, and the danger he feares,
is a harſh ſcholemaſter, to whom he is alleaging ſtill
the weakenes of the boy, and payes a fine extraordinary for his mercy. The firſt whipping rids him to the
Vniuerſity, and from thence rids him againe for feare
of ſtaruing, and the beſt he makes of him is ſome
Gull in pluſh. He is one loues to heare the famous
acts of Citizens, whereof the guilding of the Croſſe
hee counts the glory of this age: and the foure Pren-
tiſes of London aboue all the Nine Worthies. Hee
intitles himſelfe to all the merits of his Company,
whether ſchooles, Hoſpitall or exhibitions, in which
he is ioynt benefactor, though foure hundred yeere
agoe, and vpbraides them farre more then thoſe that
gaue them; yet with all this folly he has wit enough
to get wealth, and in that a sufficienter man, then he
that is wiſer.

69. *A laſciuious man*

IS the ſeruant he ſayes of many Miſtreſſes,
but all are but his luſt: to which onely hee
is faithfull, and none beſides, and ſpends
his beſt blood, and ſpirits in the ſeruice.
His ſoule is the Bawde to his body,
and thoſe that aſſiſt him in this nature, the neereſt to it. No man abuſes more the name of loue, or
thoſe whom hee applies this name to: for his loue
is like his ſtomack to feede on what he loues, and
the end of it to ſurfet and loath: till a freſh appetite
rekindle him: and it kindles on any ſooner, then who

deferue beft of him. There is a great deale of
malignity in this vice, for it loues ftil to fpoile the beft
things, and a virgin fometimes rather then beauty,
becaufe the vndoing here is greater, and confequently
his glorie. No man laughs more at his finne then he,
or is fo extremely tickled with the remembrance of
it · and he is more violence to a modeft eare, then to
her he deflowrd. A bawdy ieft enters deepe into him,
and whatfoeuer you fpeak, he will draw to bawdry,
and his witte is neuer fo good as here. His vn-
chafteft part is his tongue, for that commits alwayes,
what hee muft act feldomer: and that commits with
al, which he acts with few: for he is his own worft
reporter, and men beleeue as bad of him, and yet doe
not beleeue him. Nothing harder to his perfwafion,
then a chafte man, no Eunuch, and makes a fcoffing
miracle at it, if you tell him of a maid. And from
this miftruft it is that fuch men feare marriage, or at
leaft marry fuch as are of bodies to be trufted, to
whom onely they fell that luft which they buy of
others, and make their wife a reuennew to their Miftris.
They are men not eafily reformed, becaufe they are fo
little ill-perfwaded of their illneffe, and haue fuch pleas
from Man and Nature. Befides it is a ieering, and
flouting vice, and apt to put iefts on the reproouer.
The pox onely conuerts them, and that onely when it
kills them.

70. *A rafh man*

IS a man too quicke for himfelfe: one
whofe actions put a leg ftill before his
iudgement and out-run it. Euery hot
fancy or paffion is the fignall that fets
him forward: and his reafon comes ftill in
the reare. One that has braine enough, but not
patience to difgeft a bufineffe, and ftay the leafure of a
fecond thought. All deliberation is to him a kind of
floth, and freezing of action, and it fhall burne him

rather then take cold. Hee is alwaies refolu'd at firſt
[thinking], and the ground hee goes vpon is *hap what
may*. Thus hee enters not, but throwes himſelfe violently vpon all things, and for the moſt part is as violently throwne [vpon all] off againe: and as an obſtinate
I will was the preface to his vndertaking: ſo his concluſion is commonly *I would I had not*, for ſuch men
ſeldome do any thing, that they are not forc'd to take in
pieces againe, and are ſo much furder off from doing it,
as they haue done already. His friends are with him
as his Phyſicions: fought to onely in his ſickeneſſe, and
extremity, and to helpe him out of that mire hee has
plungd himſelfe into, for in the ſuddenneſſe of his
paſſions hee would heare nothing, and now his ill
ſucceſſe has allayd him, hee heares too late. He is
a man ſtill ſwayed with the firſt reports, and no man
more in the power of a pickthank then he. He is
one will fight firſt, and then expoſtulate; condemne
firſt, and then examine. He loſes his friend in a fit
of quarrelling, and in a fit of kindneſſe vndoes himſelfe: and then curſes the occaſion drew this mischiefe vpon him, *and cryes God mercy for it*, and curſes
againe. His repentance is meerly a rage againſt
himſelfe, and hee does ſomething in it ſtill to be re-
pented againe. Hee is a man whom fortune muſt
goe againſt much to make him happy, for had hee
beene ſufferd his owne way, hee had beene yndone.

71. *An affected man*

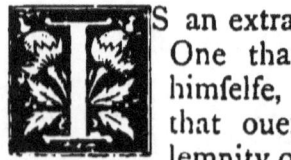S an extraordinary man, in ordinary things.
One that would goe a ſtraine beyond
himſelfe, and is taken in it. A man
that ouer-does all things with great ſo-
lemnity of circumſtance; and whereas with
more negligence he might paſſe better, makes himſelfe, with a great deale of endeuour, ridiculous. The
fancy of ſome odde quaintneſſes haue put him cleane
beſide his Nature, hee cannot bee that hee would, and

hath loſt what he was. He is one muſt be point-blank in euery trifle, as if his credit, and opinion hung vpon it: the very ſpace of his armes in an embrace ſtudied before, and premeditated: and the figure of his countenance, of a fortnights contriuing. Hee will not curſe you without booke, and *extempore*, but in ſome choiſe way, and perhaps as ſome Great man curſes. Euery action of his, *cryes, doe yee marke mee?* and men doe marke him, how abſurd he is. For affectation is the moſt betraying humour: and nothing that puzzles a man leſſe to find out then this. All the actions of his life are like ſo many things bodg'd in without any naturall cadence, or connexion at all. You ſhall track him all thorow like a ſchoole-boyes Theame, one piece from one author, and this from another, and ioyne all in this generall, that they are none of his owne: You ſhall obſerue his mouth not made for that tone, nor his face for that ſimper: And it is his lucke that his fineſt things moſt miſ-become him. If hee affect the Gentleman, as the humour moſt commonly lyes that way: not the leaſt *puntilio* of a fine man, but hee is ſtrict in to a haire, euen to their very negligences which he cons as rules: He will not carry a knife with him to wound reputation, and pay double a reckoning rather then ignobly queſtion it. And he is full of this *Ignobly* and *Nobly* and *Gentilely*, and this meer[e] feare to treſpaſſe againſt the *Gentill* way, puts him out moſt of al. It is a humour runs thorow many things beſides, but is an il-fauourd oſtentation in all, and thriues not. And the beſt vſe of ſuch men is, that they are good parts in a play.

72. *A prophane man*

IS one that denies God as farre as the Law giues him leaue, that is, onely does not ſay ſo in downeright Termes, for ſo farre he may goe. A man that does the greateſt ſinnes calmely, and as the ordinary

actions of life, and as calmely difcourfes of it againe.
Hee will tell you his bufineffe is to breake fuch a Commandement, and the breaking of the Commandement
fhall tempt him to it. His words are but fo many
vomitings caft vp to the lothfomneffe of the hearers,
onely thofe of his company loath it not. He will
take vpon him with oathes to pelt fome tenderer man
out of his company, and makes good fport at his
conqueft o're the Puritan foole. The Scripture fup-
plies him for iefts, and hee reades it of purpofe to
be thus merry. He will prooue you his fin out of
the Bible, and then aske if you will not take that
Authority. He neuer fees the Church but of purpofe
to fleepe in it: or when fome filly man preaches with
whom he means to make fport, and is moft iocund
in the Church. One that nick-names Clergymen
with all the termes of reproch, as *Rat, Black-coate*, and
the like which he will be fure to keepe vp, and neuer
calls them by other. That fing[s] Pfalmes when he is
drunke, and cryes God mercy in mockerie; for hee
muft doe it. Hee is one feemes to dare God in all
his actions, but indeed would out-dare the opinion of
him, which would elfe turne him defperate: for
Atheifme is the refuge of fuch finners, whofe repentance would bee onely to hang themfelues.

73. *A Coward*

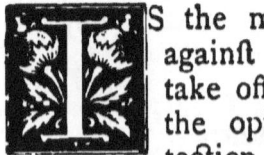S the man that is commonly moft fierce
againft the Coward, and labouring to
take off this fufpition from himfelfe: for
the opinion of valour is a good protection to thofe that dare not vfe it. No
man is valianter then he in ciuill company, and where
he thinkes no danger may come on it, and is the
readieft man to fall vpon a drawer, and thofe that
muft not ftrike againe. Wonderfull exceptious and
cholerick where he fees men are loth to giue him
occafion, and you cannot pacify him better then by

quarrelling with him. The hotter you grow, the more temperate man is hee, he protests hee alwaies honour'd you, and the more you raile vpon him, the more he honours you, and you threaten him at last into a very honest quiet man. The sight of a sword wounds him more sensibly then the stroke, for before that come hee is dead already. Euery man is his master that dare beate him, and euery man dares that knowes him. And he that dare doe this, is the onely man can doe much with him: for his friend hee cares not for, as a man that carries no such terror as his enemy, which for this cause onely is more potent with him of the two. And men fall out with him of purpose to get courtesies from him, and be brib'd againe to a reconcilement. A man in whom no secret can be bound vp, for the apprehension of each danger loosens him, and makes him bewray both the roome and it. Hee is a Christian meerely for feare of hell fire, and if any Religion could fright him more, would bee of that.

74. *A sordid rich man*

IS a begger of a faire estate: of whose wealth wee may say as of other mens vnthriftinesse, that it has brought him to this: when hee had nothing, hee liu'd in another kind of fashion. He is a man whom men hate in his owne behalfe, for vsing himselfe thus, and yet being vpon himselfe, it is but iustice; for he deserues it. Euery accession of a fresh heape bates him so much of his allowance, and brings him a degree neerer staruing. His body had beene long since desperate, but for the reparation of other mens tables, where he hoords meate in his belly for a month, to maintaine him in hunger so long. His clothes were neuer young in our memory: you might make long Epocha's from them, and put them into the Almanack with the deare yeere, and the great frost, and he is

knowne by them longer then his face. He is one
neuer gaue almes in his life, and yet is as charitable
to his Neighbour as himfelfe. Hee will redeeme a
penny with his reputation, and lofe all his friends to
boote: and his reafon, is he will not be vndone. He
neuer payes anything, but with ftrictneffe of law, for
feare of which onely hee fteales not. Hee loues to
pay fhort a fhilling or two in a great fum, and is glad
to gain that, when he can no more. He neuer fees
friend but in a iourney, to faue the charges of an Inne,
and then onely is not ficke: and his friends neuer fee
him, but to abufe him. He is a fellow indeed of a
kind of frantick thrift, and one of the ftrangeft things
that wealth can worke.

75. *A meere great man*

IS fo much Heraldrie without honour: himfelfe leffe reall than his Title. His vertue
is that hee was his Fathers fon, and all
the expectation of him to beget another.
A man that liues meerely to preferve
anothers memorie, and let vs know who died fo many
yeeres agoe. One of iuft as much vfe as his Images:
onely he differs in this that hee can fpeake himfelfe,
and faue the fellow of Weftminfter a labour: and hee
remembers nothing better then what was out of his
life: His Grandfather and their acts are his difcourfe,
and he tells them with more glory then they did them,
and it is well they did enough, or els he had wanted
matter. His other ftudies are his fports, and thofe
vices that are fit for Great men. Every vanity of his
ha's his officer, and is a ferious imployment for his
feruants. Hee talkes loud and baudily, and scurvily,
as a part of ftate, and they heare him with reverence.
All good qualities are below him, and efpecially learning except fome parcels of the Chronicle, and the
writing of his name, which hee learnes to write, not to
be read. Hee is meerely of his feruants faction and

their inſtrument for their friends and enemies, and is alwaies leaſt thankt for his owne courteſies. They that foole him moſt, doe moſt with him, and hee little thinkes how many laugh at him, barehead. No man is kept in ignorance more of himſelfe and men, for he heares nought but flatterie, and what is fit to bee ſpoken: truth with ſo much preface, that it loſes it ſelfe. Thus hee lives till his Tombe bee made ready, and is then a graue Statue to poſterity.

76. *A poore man*

IS the moſt impotent man: though neither blind nor lame, as wanting the more neceſſary limmes of life, without which limmes are a burden. A man vnfenc't and vnſhelterd from the guſts of the world, which blow all in vpon him, like an vn-rooft houſe: and the bittereſt thing hee ſuffers, is his neighbours. All men put on to him a kind of churliſher faſhion, and euen more plauſible natures churliſh to him: who are as nothing aduantg'd by his opinion. Whom men fall out with beforehand to preuent friendſhip, and his friends too, to preuent ingagements, or if they owne him, 'tis in priuate, and a by-roome, and on condition not to know them before company. All vice put together, is not halfe ſo ſcandalous, nor ſets off our acquaintance further, and euen thoſe that are not friends for ends, doe not loue any dearenneſſe with ſuch men: The leaſt courteſies are vpbraided to him, and himſelfe thank't for none: but his beſt ſeruices ſuſpected, as handſome ſharking, and tricks to get money. And wee ſhall obſerue it in knaues themſelues, that your beggerlieſt knaues are the greateſt, or thought ſo at leaſt, for thoſe that haue witte to thriue by it, haue art not to ſeeme ſo. Now a poore man has not vizard enough to maske his vices, nor ornament enough to ſet forth his vertues: but both are naked and vnhandſome: and though no man is neceſſitated to more ill, yet no mans ill is leſſe excuſ'd, but it is thought a kind of impudence in him to be vitious, and a preſumption aboue his fortune. His good parts lye dead vpon his hands, for want of matter to employ them, and at the beſt are not commended, but pittied, as vertues ill plac't: and we say of him, *'Tis an honest man, but 'tis pitty:* and yet thoſe that call him ſo, will truſt a knaue before him. Hee is a man that has the trueſt ſpeculation of the world, becauſe all men ſhew to him in their plaineſt, and worſt, as a man they haue no plot on, by appearing good to: whereas rich men are entertaind with a more holly-day behauiour, and ſee onely the beſt we can diſſemble. Hee is the onely hee that tries the true ſtrength of wiſedome, what it can doe of it ſelfe without the helpe of fortune: that with a great deale of vertue Conquers extremityes, and with a great deale more his owne impatience, and obtaines of himſelf not to hate men.

77. *An ordinairie honeſt fellow*

IS one whom it concerns to be call'd honeſt, for if he were not this, he were nothing; and yet he is not this neither: But a good dull vicious fellow, that complyes well with the deboſhments of the time, and is fit for it: One that ha's no good part in him to offend his company, or make him to bee ſuſpected a proud fellow: but is ſociably a dunce, and ſociably a drinker. That do it's faire and aboue boord without legerdemaine, and neither ſharkes for a cup nor a reckoning. That is kinde o're his beere, and proteſts he loues you, and beginnes to you againe, and loues you againe. One that quarrells with no man, but for not pledging him, but takes all abſurdities, and commits as many, and is no tell-tale next morning though hee remember it. One that will fight for his friend if hee heare him abuſed, and his friend commonly is he that is moſt likely, and hee lifts vp many a Iug in his defence. Hee railes againſt none but cenſurers, againſt whom he thinkes he railes lawfully, and cenſurers are all thoſe that are better then himſelfe. Theſe good properties qualifie him for honeſty enough, and raiſe him high in the Ale-houſe commendation, who, if he had any other good quality, would bee named by that. But now for refuge he is an honeſt man, and hereafter a ſot: Onely thoſe that commend him, thinke not ſo, and thoſe that commend him, are honeſt fellowes.

[CHARACTER FIRST FOUND IN SIXTH EDITION, 1633.]

78. *A Suſpitious, or Iealous Man*

S one that watches himſelfe a miſchiefe, and keepes a leare eye ſtill, for feare it ſhould eſcape him. A man that ſees a great deale more in every thing then is to be ſeene, and yet he thinkes he ſees nothing: His owne eye ſtands in his light. He is a fellow commonly guilty of ſome weakneſſes, which he might conceale if hee were careleſſe: Now his over-diligence to hide them, makes men pry the more. Howſoever hee imagines you have found him, and it ſhall goe hard but you muſt abuſe him whether you wil or no. Not a word can bee ſpoke, but nips him ſomewhere: not a jeſt throwne out, but he will make it hitt him; You ſhall have him goe fretting out of company, with ſome twenty quarrels to every man, ſtung and gall'd, and no man knowes leſſe the occaſion then they that have given it. To laugh before him is a dangerous matter, for it cannot be at any thing, but at him, and

to whifper in his company plaine confpiracy. *Hee bids you fpeake out, and hee will anfwere you,* when you thought not of him: Hee expoftulates with you in paffion, why you fhould abufe him, and explaines to your ignorance wherein, and gives you very good reafon, at laft, to laugh at him hereafter. He is one ftill accufing others when they are not guilty, and defending himfelfe, when hee is not accufed: and no man is undone more with Apologies, wherein he is fo elaborately exceffive, that none will beleeve him, and he is never thought worfe of, then when he ha's given fatisfaction: Such men can never have friends, becaufe they cannot truft fo farre: and this humour hath this infection with it, it makes all men to them fufpitious: In conclufion, they are men alwayes in offence and vexation with themfelves and their neighbours, wronging others in thinking they would wrong them, and themfelves moft of all, in thinking they deferve it.

www.ingramcontent.com/pod-product-compliance
Lightning Source LLC
Chambersburg PA
CBHW030409170426
43202CB00010B/1547